SURVIVING THE MONEY JUNGLE

A Junior High Study in
Handling Money
TEACHER'S GUIDE

Larry Burkett

Christian Financial Concepts, Inc.
601 Broad Street, SE
Gainesville, GA 30501

Surviving the Money Jungle—Teacher's Guide
© 1990, 1995 by Larry Burkett

Revised from *God's Guide Through the Money Jungle* by Larry Burkett. Copyright © 1985 by Christian Financial Concepts.

Printed in the United States of America.

Larry Burkett, Surviving the Money Jungle
Summary: A course for junior high young people on managing personal finances according to biblical principles.

ISBN 1-56427-070-X

Christian Financial Concepts, Inc.

0295 CFC Edition

CONTENTS

Introduction

Lessons:

INTRODUCTION

It's never too soon for young people to learn how to handle money. If money didn't matter to their happiness and purpose in the world, we wouldn't need to care. If it was their own to use, lose, or abuse as they pleased, we could allow them to find out how to handle it by trial and error.

But the fact is that all resources belong to the Lord and we are His stewards. Our purpose and happiness in life is very closely linked to how we manage what He has entrusted to us. If we do so wisely, we can enjoy the rewards of serving our Lord and His commendation: "Well done, good and faithful servant." If our management is sloppy, aimless, or selfish, our life will be filled with misery.

There are approximately 700 direct references to money in the Bible and hundreds more indirect references. Nearly two-thirds of all of Christ's parables deal with the use of money. Our use of money is closely connected to our commitment to Him.

In teaching this course, you have the opportunity in teaching a group of young people some of the most important things they will ever learn.

The Mechanics of Teaching

Each lesson is designed to fit in a sixty-minute period. There are suggested times for the various steps and activities. If you must complete the lesson in less time, pace yourself accordingly. In most cases it is better to cut the activities short than miss the last one, as it is often an important step in applying the lesson's truths.

The lessons have sections where you will be instructed to "Share the following" or "Give the following lecture." Feel free to communicate this material in whatever way is easiest for you. If you can teach it spontaneously, that's fine. If you feel more comfortable reading them, they are usually short enough that you shouldn't lose your student's attention.

Facilities and Materials

- Attempt to have a classroom where the chairs can be turned and separated into clusters for small group work.
- Each student will need a Student Workbook. Be sure to order an extra workbook or two to make visitors or new students feel welcome.
- You will also need your own copy of the Student Workbook.
- Each lesson involves some Bible study. Therefore, have extra Bibles for those students who fail to bring theirs.

• You will need a chalkboard and chalk for use in several lessons.

Advance Preparation

Each lesson includes a section listing any special supplies or arrangements you must make before the lesson. However, some lessons require long-range preparations. Turn to the following lessons to discover the arrangements you will need to make.

Lesson 3—Photocopy the "Role-play Lines" at the end of Activity 4 for the "On-the-Job Role-plays."

Lesson 6—From your local library check out a copy of James Thurber's, *Further Fables for Our Time*, or some other collection that includes the tale of "The Mouse and the Money."

Lesson 9—Rent *Mary Poppins* on video and have a VCR and monitor ready for use in your classroom. Also plan an after-class party at your home.

Lesson 10—Invite a guest speaker from your congregation to give a testimony concerning tithing.

Lesson 11—If you do not have any brochures or newsletters from denominational relief or mission organizations, send for some from organizations such as World Vision, World Concern or Food for the Hungry. See page 61.

Lesson 12—Arrange for a field trip/service project at a shelter for the homeless, soup kitchen, or rescue mission.

Perspective on the Content

For too long we have pretended that Christians have no financial problems. That's nonsense! We are subject to the same temptations as nonbelievers. But God offers great blessings to those who follow His plan. How can young people experience His blessing if they don't understand His plan? This course is your opportunity to help them learn principles that will bring life-long peace to their area of finances.

But remember, these are God's principles, not His laws. While there are consequences to not following God's counsel, He will not punish anyone for violations.

Many Christians have lived by these principles all their lives and have received the blessings God promised for obedience to them. However, some have not understood their scriptural basis. Therefore, they were unable to transfer their knowledge to others—sometimes not even to their own children. This study will help you share the concepts on a scripturally sound basis.

THIS WAY TO FREEDOM

Advance Preparation:

If you expect your class to be over ten or twelve, enlist the aid of an assistant who can help you monitor student work during the exercises where they are asked to work individually or in small groups. Your assistant should also have a Leader's Guide and Student Text.

Make sure that your classroom has—

☐ chairs that can be easily turned and clustered for small group interaction;

☐ a chalkboard or overhead projector to assist in presenting information to the group as well as recording responses from the group.

Letter the following survey questions on the chalkboard or an overhead transparency:

• Do you receive an allowance?

• Can you do anything you want to with it? Or is all or some of it designated for such things as clothes, school lunches, bus fare, etc.?

• Do you do irregular odd jobs (baby-sitting, yard work, etc.) for which you get paid? If so, about how many hours per week do you work at these?

• Do you have a regular, part-time job? If so, how many hours per week do you work?

Supplies:

☐ Student Workbooks

☐ Pens or pencils

☐ Bibles

Getting Started *(10 minutes)*

Welcome the students as they arrive and call attention to the survey questions on the board or overhead. Instruct students to ask these questions of at least three other class members.

Introduce the series by sharing the following:

> Have you ever thought much about freedom? Some people think freedom is being able to do whatever you want to do when you want to do it. But let's suppose that on Saturday afternoon you are invited to go to your best friend's birthday party and also water skiing with your cousin. You're free to do either. But you can't do both because you can't be in two places at the same time.
>
> Much of life is like that. A choice to do one thing means you can't do other things. And trying to "have it both ways" can

Lesson Aim:

• To help your students compare financial bondage and financial freedom.

• To introduce your students to God's desire that every Christian will experience financial freedom.

be one of the most frustrating, "un-free" things you can do. It's that way with money.

Apparently a lot of people think that financial freedom means lots of money, expensive clothes, the ability to buy anything and everything you want. But the choice to view money that way means missing out on God's perspective. He wants you to experience financial freedom; that's for sure. But He wants you to avoid the envy, anxiety, confusion, waste, and debt that so often accompany the world's struggle for financial freedom.

As Christians, God wants to meet our needs, give us an abundance of spiritual riches (like commitment to Christ, sharing the Gospel, and families, for starters), and maybe (or maybe not) some extra money allowing us the opportunity to demonstrate our love and obedience to Him.

Perhaps this is the first time you have ever thought of this, but money is a tool God uses to test our trustworthiness. It's our responsibility to learn how to pass the test. And, that's what this Bible study is all about—following God's way to financial freedom.

STEP 1
Some Things About Money Bug Me! *(10 minutes)*

Objective: To help the students begin to identify ways in which finances worry them.

1. Have the students read through the Step 1 statements in their workbooks, checking off those that apply to them. The statements are:
   1. I worry about having enough money for summer camp, school clothes, new bike, etc.
   2. I feel like I never have enough money.
   3. I'm lost when it comes to planning a budget.
   4. I hate to spend my own money. I'd rather get money from my parents.
   5. When I go into a store, I always end up buying something. I can't "just look."
   6. I wish I didn't have to have a job.
   7. I'm bugged because I don't have as many nice things as my friends have.
   8. I always owe my parents or friends money. I guess I just forget to pay them back.
   9. It always seems like I'm the one who has money and my friends never do. They always ask me to loan them a few

dollars. I wish they'd use their own money.

10. I usually have more money than my friends. I guess I like how that makes me feel.

2. After you have allowed students a few minutes to mark the things that bug them, share one or two that are a struggle for you.

3. Ask for a show of hands of those who marked item number one, then two, etc. Choose the ones that were most frequently marked and invite volunteers to tell why they think that area is a problem. Don't embarrass anyone by forcing self-revelation.

STEP 2
Symptoms of Being Trapped by Money
(15 minutes)

Objective: To help the students realize that financial bondage does exist by helping them identify some of its symptoms.

1. Share the following:

If you're bugged about money, it could be that you're experiencing some forms of "financial bondage." Financial bondage simply means that money problems or money worries are messing up your life and your peace of mind. This is bound to happen occasionally because the temptation always exists to let material possessions interfere with our relationship to God.

You see, bondage occurs regardless of the amount of money we have. You might buy a new portable, AM/FM, cassette stereo and start showing it off to your friends, listening to tapes right after school (at the expense of homework, etc.), even start worrying that someone might steal it. That's bondage!

Or maybe you don't own a boom box like that . . . but you wish you did. So you start thinking of ways to get one. You scrimp and save every penny (maybe you even stop giving an offering at church), waiting for the day you can own a box of your own. In the meantime, you visit a friend and listen to his or her new cassette stereo. Are you jealous (just a little?) because your friends seem to get everything they want—when they want it—and you have to work for what you want?

That, too, is bondage.

There's nothing wrong with owning a boom box—unless, of course, it disrupts your relationship to God, your relationship with others, or interferes with your responsibilities. The possession itself isn't the problem. It's our attitude toward possessions that can be a problem!

2. Have the students form pairs or trios. Instruct them to turn to "Symptoms of Being Trapped by Money" in Step 2 in their workbook. Each pair or trio should correctly match the symptoms with the Bible verses that describe them:

• Dishonesty	Proverbs 28:6
• Not giving to God's work	Proverbs 3:9,10
• Too many risks, hasty decisions	Proverbs 28:20
• Overdue debts	Psalm 37:21
• Hoarding	Matthew 6:19,20
• Worry about future needs	Matthew 6:25
• Jealousy of what others have	Ephesians 5:5
• No desire to earn money	2 Thessalonians 3:10
• Wasting	Ecclesiastes 2:10,11

In the space provided in the workbook, they should write down two or three symptoms from the list and then below each one, describe in their own words a situation one person in their group has seen happen which demonstrates that particular symptom. It might be something that happened to them, a peer, or an adult.

Refer students to the example in their workbooks if they don't understand what they are to do.

For this activity there are no "right answers." It is merely designed to help the students connect the symptoms of financial bondage with real-life situations so that they can understand that financial bondage does exist.

STEP 3
Diagnosing the Problem (15 minutes)

Objective: To help the students understand that underlying the symptoms of financial bondage are deeper spiritual problems.

1. Share the following:

Sometimes things aren't exactly what they seem. Suppose you owed your parents money but weren't paying them back. You might say, "Oh, I just forgot," and that might be true, once or twice. But if you keep "forgetting," it might be because of a deeper problem. You may have a problem with self-indulgence and end up spending money on yourself that should be used to repay your debt.

Or you might be financially ignorant and not really understand your responsibility to pay back the money.

Here's another example: Suppose you stopped giving part of your allowance and earnings to your church. "They don't really appreciate my little contributions," you say to yourself. But the problem may not be a lack of appreciation in your church; you might be suffering from greed, pride, or maybe even a lack of spiritual commitment.

2. Assign individuals, pairs or trios to complete the maze in Step 3 (Diagnosing the Problem). Instruct them to read the verse(s) at each intersection and notice the deeper problem underlying any wrong turns in the route:

Psalm 73:2,3	JEALOUSY OF WEALTHY
Proverbs 11:24	GREED, SELFISHNESS
Proverbs 11:28	DEPENDING ON MONEY
Proverbs 18:9	LAZINESS
Proverbs 21:17	SELF-INDULGENCE
Proverbs 28:19b	UNREALISM, IGNORANCE,
Proverbs 28:20b	"GET-RICH-QUICK" ATTITUDE
Malachi 3:8	LACK OF SPIRITUAL COMMIT-
	MENT, DISOBEDIENCE TO GOD
1 Timothy 6:9,10	DESIRE FOR RICHES,
	PUTTING MONEY FIRST

3. Allow four or five minutes to complete the maze, then call on students to describe a specific problem as if they observed it in one of their friends. Or ask, "What damage is done to a person who has this action or attitude?"

4. Next have students move on in Step 3 and identify which underlying (inner, spiritual) problems may cause specific symptoms. Call attention to the two completed examples in their workbooks. Then invite volunteers to suggest the probable inner problems which cause each of the other symptoms listed.

Again, this is not an exercise with right or wrong answers. However, if the class gets stuck, here are some suggested answers:

• Overdue debts—financial ignorance, selfishness, putting the wrong things first, greed, poor planning, etc.
• Not giving to God's work—lack of spiritual commitment, greed, selfishness
• Dishonesty—greed, pride

- Too many risks, hasty decisions—"get-rich-quick" attitude, greed
- Wasting—laziness, greed, pride
- Hoarding—financial ignorance, selfishness, putting wrong things first, lack of spiritual commitment
- Worry about future needs—financial ignorance, selfishness, putting wrong things first
- Jealous of what others have—greed, putting wrong things first
- No desire to earn money—laziness, financial ignorance, selfishness

STEP 4
The Road to Financial Freedom (10 minutes)

Objective: To evaluate your students' understanding of the difference between financial bondage and financial freedom as a preview of what is to come in the rest of the course.

1. Have your students discuss the following four questions, writing their answers in their workbooks. Listen for whether they are beginning to understand the difference between financial bondage and financial freedom.

   1. What do you think Ecclesiastes 5:10 means when it says: "Whoever loves money never has money enough; whoever loves wealth is never satisfied with his income. This too is meaningless." (Money and the things money can buy can never bring lasting satisfaction. Wealth creates a desire for more, resulting in life with no real purpose.)
   2. And what do you think Deuteronomy 8:18 means? ("But remember the LORD your God, for it is he who gives you the ability to produce wealth, and so confirms his covenant.")
   3. Do you think every Christian should have lots and lots of material possessions? Why or why not? (God doesn't promise luxury to His children. He promises to meet our needs, to make us "wealthy" according to His standards, not the world's.)
   4. What are one or two things you would like to learn about money during this course?

2. Now go through the following preview of some of the highlights of future lessons. Remember, your interest in these topics will be contagious.

- In Lesson 3 you'll find out the most satisfying attitude toward work when you discover that God is your real Boss.
- Lesson 4 takes a good look at all the things you may think you own.
- How much money would it take to really satisfy you? Discover "The Secret of Contentment," in Lesson 5.
- Do you ever struggle with honesty in handling money? Lesson 8 will help you understand why God lets you face temptations
- Have you ever heard someone say, "You can't take it with you," referring to what happens to your money when you die? Well, the Bible tells how to send your treasure on ahead to be deposited in the "bank" of heaven so you can enjoy it after you die. Find out how in Lesson 9.
- Suppose a panhandler approaches you on the street and asks for a quarter. Should you give away some of your hard-earned money? Lesson 12 has some thoughtful suggestions for, "Who Deserves Help."

GOODBYE, MONEY WORRIES!

Advance Preparation:

☐ Think carefully of some concrete financial worries that you have now or have experienced in the past that you can share with your students in Activity 1. As your students see your vulnerability, they'll be more willing to share their fears, as well.

☐ Read through the story in Activity 3 aloud so that you can do so smoothly during class.

Lesson Aim:
- To help your students identify their personal money worries.
- To build trust in God by seeing how God uses money in concrete ways.

Supplies:

☐ Student Workbooks
☐ Pencils or pens
☐ Bibles
☐ Large newsprint or butcher paper
☐ Felt markers

Getting Started (5 minutes)

Provide a large sheet of newsprint or butcher paper. Either mount it on a wall or bulletin board or spread it on a table or on the floor. Letter across the top: "Common Money Worries." Place several felt markers by the sheet.

As students arrive, ask them to each write at least one typical money worry they have noticed bothering people.

Once the class has written a good number of worries, ask the group to vote for the ones they feel are most common. Make tally marks beside each item for which students vote.

Introduce this topic by calling attention to the workbook statement of what students will learn in this lesson.

STEP 1
I Sometimes Worry (15 minutes)

Objective: To get your students to think in specifics about the kinds of financial concerns that worry them.

1. Introduce Step 1 in the workbooks by sharing some financial worry you have now or have had. Make it real, but keep it on a level that they will understand.

2. Instruct students to complete the first statement: "I wish I could afford...because...."

   The extent you urge the students to share their answers

should be modified by the general degree of trust within the group and the relatively similar backgrounds from which they come. For instance, you could be encouraging cruel ridicule if you press a poor student to share that he wishes he could afford new shoes. Evaluate your group's ability to handle information sensitively.

Answers to question #2 might include—
- Borrowing excessively
- Becoming stingy
- Working two jobs
- Stealing
- Cheating

3. Question three is pretty personal and need not be shared. Point out that most people who have never given this subject much thought will mark answers that show some uncertainty about whether they really trust God to provide for them. This recognition leads directly into a very helpful Bible study: God's Answers to Money Worries.

STEP 2
God's Answers to Money Worries (10 minutes)

Objective: To help your students understand that God knows our situation, and He has everything under control.

1. Ask a volunteer to read Matthew 6:25-34. Point out that the verses don't mention money, but they deal with the reasons we need money. Have the students answer the questions in their workbook. Their answers will likely be similar to the following:

   1. Have faith in God. Try to do what God wants you to do. He will take care of all your needs.
   2. No, because we would be doing God's will and God does not want us to be lazy. Not worrying does not mean being lazy.

STEP 3
How God Builds Our Trust (20 minutes)

Objective: To help the students understand that our trust in God grows as we experience His faithfulness in smaller things.

1. Invite a discussion of why we have trouble trusting God. Some answers might be as follows:

   - Maybe we lack confidence in God's love.

- Maybe we lack confidence in His power.
- If we don't believe God cares about our needs, we'll naturally trust our own efforts more than we'll trust God's promises.

2. Point out that trust doesn't grow in a vacuum. We learn to trust someone because he proves himself trustworthy. God understands that. He longs to demonstrate His trustworthiness to all His children.

3. Read aloud the following story about trust.

> Imagine that one day a man knocks on your door. When you answer, he says, "I'm going to give you $50 in two weeks." He then leaves you his card and shuts the door.
>
> You think, "How strange that was." Then you start checking him out. You begin to talk to people who might know something about him.
>
> You discover that he is a multi-billionaire and that he has given thousands of dollars to people. Knowing this, your confidence in him grows. But, still, you don't have any real trust in him because he hasn't given you any money.
>
> However, in two weeks he returns and delivers the $50. Your trust in him suddenly grows.
>
> Then, he says, "I've decided to give you $1,000 in two more weeks."
>
> You already know that he is a multi-billionaire, so you know he has the resources, and he has already given you $50. But $1,000 is so much more. Why would anyone give away that much? Then, in talking to other people, you discover that this man has occasionally given away that much in the past. You also discover something else: Everyone who knows him says that he has never lied—no matter what. When he says that he's going to do something, he always does it.
>
> In two weeks, he returns and hands you the $1,000. Now your trust really grows. Over the next few months, he continues to give you more and more money! Each time your trust in him grows.
>
> Then one day he comes to you after being away for some time and says, "In three months I will give you $100,000."
>
> Well, by this time you have absolute confidence in him. You know exactly how he operates. You know that he has the funds, and you know that once he says something, it will be done. You also learn that he has given hundreds of thousands of dollars to other people as well. And so

with full confidence, you can plan how you are going to spend that money, knowing he's going to deliver exactly what he promises.

4. Explain that trust in God is very similar to this story:

When God promises us things, He promises them through His Word. And the Bible has in it everything that God will ever do for us. As we read it, we begin to understand that God indeed is the owner of everything. When He says He can supply things, He can. In talking to others, we find that what God promises in Scripture, He delivers.

He begins by giving small things at first, because we are only capable of trusting Him for small things. But as He gives us small things, our confidence in Him grows, and the more He is able to supply. Thus God can use money to demonstrate His power to us.

5. Have the students answer the questions in their workbooks.

STEP 4
Practical Lessons in Trust (10 minutes)

Objective: To plan practical ways to build trust in God.

1. Lead the students in working individually to complete the "I Would Like to Trust God" activity in their workbooks.
2. After several minutes, lead a time of individual prayer about the items listed.
3. Encourage the students to complete the practical steps in building trust. If time permits, invite volunteerss to share one action they plan to take.

GOD IS MY BOSS

Advance Preparation:

☐ Make a photocopy of the "On the Job Role-plays" from the last page of this lesson and cut the three situations apart for use in Activity 4.

☐ Roll out an eight- to ten-foot length of shelf paper. Mount it along a wall, on a table top or on the floor. Across the top letter, "Job Ranking Chart." Then divide the chart into seven sections a shown below:

Lesson Aim:
- To help your students evaluate their attitude toward their jobs (whether they are chores, homework, or other employment);
- To identify why it is important to work with excellence, diligence, and humility—for God's glory.

JOB RANKING CHART						
Disgusting	Depressing	Boring	OK	Interesting	Exciting	Glamorous
(LOW PAY						HIGH PAY)

Supplies:

☐ Student Workbooks
☐ Bibles
☐ Pencils or pens
☐ Small index cards for Getting Started and Step 4 activities
☐ Masking tape or cellophane tape

Getting Started (10 minutes)

As students arrive, instruct them to write with felt markers on separate small index cards the jobs they now do or have done. Then they are to place (using tape) each card on the section of the Job Ranking Chart which they feel best fits each job. If several students place the same job in different parts of the chart, ask them to explain their evaluations.

When the chart is complete, comment on the students' placement of their tasks:

> Sometimes we feel like work is a cruel punishment, but it's not. It's a gift from God. The wise King Solomon once said, "I know that there is nothing better for men than to be happy and do good . . ., that everyone may eat and drink and find satisfaction in all his toil—this is the gift of God" (Ecclesiastes 3:12,13).

Point to the jobs on the low end of the chart. Ask, "Why would Solomon call these jobs 'gifts of God'?" Encourage various students to respond.

Next, ask "What would your attitude toward one of these low-end jobs be if you knew God had provided that task as a good gift for you?" After several students reply, ask, "What difference would it make to also know that your boss for those jobs was God, Himself?"

Well, guess what? God IS your real boss.

STEP 1
Boss for a Day (10 minutes)

Objective: To help your students realize that God is with us in all situations.

1. Pose this situation to the students:

> Imagine that the next time you went to mow your neighbor's lawn, your neighbor announced, "I'm leaving for the rest of the day. I'd like you to meet the supervisor who will take my place while I'm gone—Jesus Christ."
> Sure enough! Jesus Christ is there to see how well you do and oversee the yard work for the day.

2. Allow time for the students to answer the questions in their workbooks. Then discuss with them their answers and their feelings about the notion of Jesus being their boss. Many students may feel intimidated at the thought of having Jesus for their boss. Admit that you, too, have these feelings. Talk a few minutes about them. Point out that while it is true that God is present with us at all times, He is also understanding. Therefore, while we need to do our best, we don't need to fear not being good enough.

STEP 2
"As Working for the Lord" (10 minutes)

Objective: To help your students understand that "working for the Lord" means doing the very best we can, even if nobody is watching or rewards us.

1. Ask students, "What do you think it means to 'work as for the Lord'?" (To do your work realizing that God is your true boss; do every part of the job to please Him.)
2. Have students look up the Scriptures and identify the principles from the second part of this activity. Instruct them to unscramble the words to discover the definitions of each principle.

- Principle 1 (from Proverbs 10:4; 13:4 and Colossians 3:23): Diligence. It means: Working hard and efficiently.
- Principle 2 (from Numbers 18:29 and 1 Peter 4:11): Excellence. It means: Doing the best quality work you can so that God (your real boss) is honored through what you do.
- Principle 3 (from Philippians 2:3,4 and Matthew 20:25-28): Humility. It means: Not bragging about talents, but using them to help others.

3. If you have enough time, ask the students how much they see these principles in action. Why do they think they are so often rare?

STEP 3
Evaluating My Work Habits (10 minutes)

Objective: To encourage your students to honestly evaluate their own work habits and decide where they may need improvement.

1. Ask volunteers to look up and read the verses that allude to negative attitudes toward work. Allow the group to discuss and agree on what the "Principles for Failure" are. They should roughly reflect the following concepts.

   Principles for Failure

   Proverbs 19:15 — Laziness.
   Psalm 28:4 — Evil.
   Proverbs 16:5 — Pride.

2. The second question in this activity will have individual answers according to each student's situation. Allow the students a few minutes to think about the chart and mark an "X" in one box under each work area. Then have them evaluate which of the Success principles and which of the Failure principles they tend to follow most often. Don't expect the students to share their answers. (For some, an honest answer could be unhelpfully embarrassing. For others a positive answer could stimulate bragging.)

STEP 4
On the Job (20 minutes)

Objective: To encourage your students to become committed to working in a way that brings glory to God and to practice (through role-plays) how natural responses might be transformed into godly responses.

1. Most of your students probably listed at least one principle in the previous activity that doesn't please God. Encourage them that God can help them change their life so they can live by the godly principles instead. Allow the students a few minutes to write down their goal and then sign their name as a commitment before the Lord.

2. Pass out index cards for the students to write themselves a reminder of their goal to post in a prominent place in their room at home.

3. Select three pairs of students to role-play the situations on the role-play cards you duplicated and cut out. Read aloud the first situation printed below, and then hand the "boss" the card with his or her lines to read "with feeling." Then the "worker" should answer in the way that would come most naturally. The boss and worker continue to ad-lib the next several verbal exchanges.

4. Next, have the students change roles. The new boss should read his or her lines, but this time the new worker should respond as though he or she were working directly for God. Allow for additional ad-libbed exchanges. Then ask the class to discuss the role-play. (Do this for each of the role-play situations.)

- Was the first "natural" response similar to how the students might have answered?
- In real life, what would have been the result of such a response?
- Was the second response realistic? With God's help, could someone have actually responded that way?

The answers your young people give to these questions may reveal a lot about their understanding of God. On one extreme some kids may see God as a tyrant against whom they are inclined to rebel. On the other extreme, God may seem too unapproachable to hear them if they respectfully request some kind of variance, etc. This may be a time for some important teaching on the nature of God.

Situation 1, Chores

You and three of your friends have planned to go to the beach Saturday. Almost everything is lined up. One of the other kid's parents will drive you and pick you up. Your friends have each given you three dollars for food, and you're to do the shopping before noon when you all plan to leave. There's just one thing. You haven't mentioned the plan to your folks. And since everyone in your family is expected to do chores together on Saturday mornings, you'll need to be excused from that responsibility today.

It's Saturday morning at breakfast. Your dad says. . .

Situation 2, Homework

You worked extra hard on your book report. To begin with, the book was twice as long as usual, and you even did some extra research on the author. Last night you neglected to work on a huge social studies assignment that is due in two days just so you could finish the book report on time. You're hoping for a very good grade.

Just as the bell rings your teacher asks to speak to you for a moment before you leave.

Situation 3, Baby-sitting

The Carlsens are your lowest paying baby-sitting customer. But they are regular, and usually their two-year-old is in bed asleep when you arrive, so it's easy to use the evening as you please— watch TV, call a friend, or finish your homework.

Tonight you hurry over with an armload of books. Because you were sick earlier this week, you're going to have to spend all evening catching up tonight. But at least you have a nice quiet place to work. When you arrive. . .

More Questions for Thought:

If you have time, discuss the following.

1. What do you think it means to glorify God?
2. Why do you think God wants to be glorified through your work?
3. Most people work primarily to make money. Why do you (or why don't you) think this is the best motivation for working? (It is not wrong to make money; it is a good, necessary thing for everyone to do. As Christians we must not allow earning money to get in the way of our higher calling: to serve God and others.)

On the Job Role-play Lines

————————————————— CUT HERE —————————————————

Situation 1, Chores

Father: It's getting near the end of summer. If we don't get started painting the garage today, we're going to get caught by wet weather before we're finished.

Therefore, for this morning's work, as soon as we finish eating, I'd like all of us to get started on scraping and priming. We've got a lot to do.

————————————————— CUT HERE —————————————————

Situation 2, Homework

Teacher: I was flipping through the book reports when I noticed how nice yours looked. However, didn't you remember that this was supposed to be a book report on a contemporary biography? What you read was a mystery.

I'll tell you what, I'll grant you a one-week extension to turn in a report on a contemporary biography.

————————————————— CUT HERE —————————————————

Situation 3, Baby-sitting

Mrs. Carlsen: Oh, I'm so glad you arrived a few minutes early. I want you to meet Shelley—she's eight; and Marcie—she's six; and Philip—he's five. My sister and her family are staying with us for a few days, and we're just dying for a chance for us adults to all get out of the house for the evening.

I meant to call you about the extra kids. Sorry; we'll pay you a little extra.

We'll probably be back a little late, but don't worry about putting the older kids down. They can stay up. Try to keep them from getting too loud, though. I'm afraid they might wake the baby. That happened last night, and it was hours before I could get him back to sleep.

————————————————————————————————

TAKIN' CARE OF BUSINESS

Background:

O f all the concepts presented in this course, the recognition that God is owner and we are stewards is the most significant. A young person who comes to grips with this truth will find all other financial decisions easier to make.

Advance Preparation:

☐ Study Step 4 which leads the students to personally surrender to the Lord all they have. If you have non-Christian students in your class, this could lead to their basic commitment to Jesus. Take the time to review how to lead someone to the Lord so you are prepared should this happen.

☐ Also, if you have not already done so, it might be useful to recruit an assistant for this session or make other arrangements so that you would be free to talk privately with any non-Christians who are open to the Gospel.

☐ Prepare the following five mini-posters, boldly lettering the text on sheets of colored paper:
1. Give it away to someone.
2. Ask a good friend to care for it until you get back.
3. Ask a stranger to care for it until you get back.
4. Ask someone who doesn't like you to care for until you get back.
5. Pay someone to care for it until you get back.
Mount the posters around the room.

Supplies:

☐ Student Workbooks
☐ Bibles
☐ Pencils or pens
☐ Index cards

Lesson Aim:

• To help your students describe the difference between a "steward's" attitude toward possessions and an "owner's" attitude.

Getting Started (10 minutes)

As students arrive, tell them, "Imagine you have a very valuable pet which needs special care. You are going away for a month and need to provide for your pet. Choose one of the five options on the posters around the room and write on an index card why you chose it."

Collect the cards and group them by the five options. Read some of the cards aloud. Most students probably chose Option #2. Ask, "Do you think your pet would get better care from a new owner or from a friend doing you a favor? Why?" It is not necessary to resolve the issue, just to get students thinking about some possible differences in these situations.

Point out that this session shows that we are like the good friend caring for God's possessions. The Bible calls us "stewards."

> A steward is "someone who manages another's property." When the Bible says we are stewards of our money and possessions, it is saying we do not own them—we are merely managing them for the real owner, who is God. "The earth is the Lord's, and everything in it" (Psalm 24:1).
>
> The issue is, when you're "takin' care of business," whose business are you taking care of? Do you think of yourself as a steward of God's business or the owner of your own business?

STEP 1
Whose Business Is It, Anyway? (15 minutes)

Objective: To help the students come to the rather challenging insight that nothing they have is of their own making. Everything has been entrusted (given) to them, ultimately from God.

1. Introduce this segment of the study:

   > The apostle Paul helps us understand the role of a steward in his first letter to the Corinthians where he wrote:
   >
   > "Let a man regard us in this manner, as servants of Christ, and stewards of the mysteries of God. In this case, moreover, it is required of stewards that one be found trustworthy. . . . And what do you have that you did not receive?" (1 Corinthians 4:1,2,7b NASB).

2. Ask, "What do you have that you did not receive from someone else?" In their workbooks have them make a list of things that they generated totally on their own. They should not include anything that was given to them or that they obtained by trading something that was originally given to them. In the next column they should write how they obtained each item.

3. After they have had a few moments to make their lists, ask them to go back over them carefully considering the history of each item. The question is, did they really earn or create it all by themselves?

4. Ask for volunteers to name things from their lists. List these on the chalkboard. Then when several things have been listed so that no individual will be singled out, go over the list in

inviting the students to discuss the following questions:

- How about the **time** required to earn or create it? Where did you get it? The Bible says God numbers our days and gives us the very breath of life.
- Where did you get the **intelligence, good looks, or strength** required? Didn't you inherit them as a gift from God and through your parents?
- Where did you get the **skills**? Didn't someone teach you?

It does not take long to see that everything we have is the result of what was given to us or what we traded that first was given to us. And ultimately the Source of all we have is God.

We know this vaguely, but in a world with an ownership mindset, even we Christians can easily get caught up in thinking that our possessions are our own to use as we please. Oh, maybe not all of them. We may admit that a tithe—ten percent of our profit—belongs to God. "But, surely," we say, "the rest is ours to use as we please!"

The Bible teaches differently. Everything we have belongs to God. None of it is ours to use as our own. All of it is to be used the way God wants it used. God is the owner; He has merely employed us as managers.

You are a steward. Whether or not you know it, whether or not you like it, you are a steward. You have no choice in the matter. God has entrusted to you certain resources—money, possessions, time, energy, abilities— and He has made you responsible to care for them, to use them to fulfill His purposes in the world. You are managing God's resources.

Some people use God's resources for their own pleasure as though they owned them. That doesn't make them non-stewards; it simply makes them poor stewards. Good stewards don't act like they own the property they manage; they manage it as the owner wishes.

To become a good steward, the first step is to accept your place as a steward—as a manager of someone else's property—and to commit yourself to managing that property totally for the owner's benefit, in the way He wants it managed.

STEP 2
A Parable of Three Stewards (15 minutes)

Objective: To teach the precepts found in Christ's parable about the talents in terms of our role as stewards of God's gifts.

1. Ask a volunteer to read Matthew 25:14-30. Make sure the students understand the story. (Bible scholars tell us that a talent was worth about a thousand dollars.)

2. Then discuss the following questions, encouraging the students to write the answers in their workbooks.

   1. Why was each servant given a separate amount? (Each had different abilities.)
   2. Did the owner expect each servant to earn the same amount? (No, the owner did not ask the stewards to earn the same, but he did ask them all to increase their amounts.)
   3. How were the faithful servants rewarded? (The faithful servants were put in charge of more important things.)
   4. What was done to the unfaithful servant? (The unfaithful servant was stripped of his talents.)
   5. The three servants were stewards. What is the difference between an owner and a steward? (A steward is a caretaker of the owner's things.)
   6. How does a good steward manage the property entrusted to him or her? (A good steward manages the property as the owner wants it managed.)
   7. How do we know if we are owners or stewards of our possessions? Explain your answer. (We are stewards because everything we have, God has given us to enjoy for a time—until He comes again.)
   8. What difference should this make in the way we use our money and possessions? (Our security should not be in the things but in God.)

STEP 3
Windfall! (10 minutes)

Objective: To further contrast a steward's approach to possessions with an owner's attitude.

1. The first step in developing stewardship skills is to realize that being a steward involves an attitude of stewardship. This "Windfall!" activity will help your students understand good

stewardship attitudes.

Read aloud the following scenario:

Imagine that you've just been given $500, and now you have to decide what to do with it! Based on the following instructions, develop two possible spending plans.

The "Owner" Plan
Imagine that $500 is all yours to use just as you please. How you spend it is no one else's business—not even God's. What kind of things might you do with your $500 windfall?

The "Steward" Plan
God has just entrusted you with $500 of His money for you to manage for Him. Your mission is to use the $500 in ways which please God. What kind of things might you do with the money?

2. Have the students work individually to fill out each plan in their workbooks, and then answer the questions that follow the plans.

3. After four or five minutes, invite them to compare their plans with those done by several others in the group.

4. Ask if students included anything for themselves in their Steward Plan. Help the students understand that this can be appropriate if it reflects wise spending and accompanies sharing and saving. The contrast is that in an Owner Plan, more items are likely to be self-indulgent.

STEP 4
Quit-Claim Deed (10 *minutes*)

Objective: To guide the students to make a personal commitment, surrendering all they have to the Lord, based on what they have been learning about their role as stewards of God's resources.

1. Ask a student to read aloud the "Quit-Claim Deed" printed in the Student Workbook.

2. Then, answer any questions students raise about its meaning and purpose. (It is designed so the students can sign to quit—surrender—their claim to everything they have—their money, possessions, time, energy, or abilities. The objective is to recognize that these all belong to God and that He has only entrusted them to us to manage as He directs.

3. Encourage your students to pray silently for a few minutes and ask God to show them if they are ready to sign this commitment. Emphasize that they don't have to sign it. In fact, they really shouldn't sign it if they aren't convinced that it represents the way God wants them to regard their things or if they aren't ready to do so. Encourage those who do sign it to silently pray the prayer provided in the Student Workbook.

If you happen to be working with non-Christians, this kind of a commitment represents a substantial surrender to the Lord. Any non-Christian willing to make this much of a commitment is probably ready to have the whole Gospel explained. Arrange a time (right after class, during the coming week, etc.) to meet with any such student to explain how to become a Christian.

THE SECRET OF CONTENTMENT

Advance Preparation:

Arrange the classroom so that the students can work in groups of three.

Lesson Aim:
- To lead students away from the "more is better" philosophy.
- To help students understand the benefits of moderation and trust in God's provision.

Supplies:

- ☐ Student Workbooks
- ☐ Bibles
- ☐ Pencils or pens
- ☐ Several old, secular magazines with lots of advertising
- ☐ Large sheets of paper
- ☐ Scissors
- ☐ Felt markers
- ☐ Glue

Getting Started (15 minutes)

Divide the class into groups of threes, and distribute copies of magazines. Have the students cut out ads which promise happiness through things. Have them glue the ads onto sheets of paper. They may also add slogans they remember from radio or television advertising. Here are a few samples of slogans you may suggest if students need help:

- "Everyone pursues happiness. Some people just take a more direct route." —Norwegian Cruise Line.
- "The heartbeat of America, today's Chevrolet."
- "You've come a long way, baby." —Virginia Slims.
- "It's not just your car; it's your freedom." —Mr. Goodwrench, GM Parts.
- "Hold your world together with the power of mobile communications." —GTE Airfone.
- "We've produced more happy endings than anyone in Hollywood." —The Prudential Insurance Company.
- "Everything." —Chrysler New Yorker.

After five minutes, have students display and explain the ad slogans they found.

Then share the following:

You have probably seen the bumper sticker that says: "Life is a game. Whoever dies with the most toys wins." It was meant as a joke, but unfortunately too many of us have learned to measure contentment in terms of how many dollars we make and how many "things" we can buy. By implication, those who don't have lots of things are unsuccessful. And so, the vicious cycle begins. We want more success and then, more things. And then we become even more discontent, so we buy even more!

Materialism bombards us from every angle, day in and day out. Advertisements, television, and peer pressure all promote the lie that "things" breed happiness.

In this kind of world, is it any wonder that the art of contentment seems like a well-kept secret? Fortunately for us, it's not. God's plan for every believer's finances includes contentment. This lesson is designed to help you learn contentment according to God's plan.

STEP 1
How Much Would It Take? (*5 minutes*)

Objective: To set the stage to show your students how much we are steeped in materialism.

1. Each of us has thought some time or another about what a person "needs" to be content. Ask the students to list in their workbooks what they think the typical family in your community "needs" to feel content.
2. When they have had a few minutes to make their list, ask for volunteers to share what they wrote. List their ideas on the chalkboard. (Keep this list on the board for Step 5.)
3. Ask, "Do you know any people who would be content without some of these things? Why might some people feel they need things that other people don't need?"

STEP 2
The Enemy of Contentment (*15 minutes*)

Objective: Study what Paul says in the Bible concerning the enemy of contentment.

1. Have a volunteer read aloud 1 Timothy 6:6-10.
2. Then ask the students the following questions. They should record their answers in the workbooks as they respond verbally.

   1. With what are we to be content? (Verse 8—We are to be content with food and clothes.)
   2. What happens to people who want to get rich? (Verse 9—People who want to get rich fall into temptations and

foolish and harmful desires which plunge people into ruin and destruction.)

3. What is the love of money? (Verse 10—The love of money is the root of all sorts of evil.)

4. What have some people done because they were eager for money? (Verse 10—Some people have wandered away from the faith, and have brought on themselves many disappointments and griefs.)

5. How do you think Paul would answer someone who said, "If I only had more, then I would be content"? (Paul would probably say to learn to be content with what you have. See Philippians 4:11-13.)

STEP 3
Diagnosing Discontent (5 minutes)

Objective: To help the students identify symptoms of discontent that they may have experienced.

1. Point out that many clues exist that can let us know if we are suffering from discontentment. Some are: over-commitment to earning extra money, stinginess, and defining success in material terms.

2. Instruct the students to turn to Step 3 in their workbooks and check the symptoms of discontentment that they have felt in the past.

STEP 4
Learning to Be Content (10 minutes)

Objective: To help the students comprehend the importance of living a balanced life that employs Paul's insights for being content.

1. Share the following:

How do you learn to be content? Paul learned the secret of being content in every situation—whether he had a lot or just a little. In Philippians 4:12 he said, "I know what it is to be in need, and I know what it is to have plenty. I have learned the secret of being content in any and every situation, whether well fed or hungry, whether living in plenty or in want."

Contentment is not just learning to get along without things. It's letting God make the decisions—to provide or withhold—according to what is best. And just because you can afford something doesn't mean you should buy it, either. Being content is finding a balance between having more than you need (abundance) and not having what you need (lack).

You won't be able to master the secret of contentment overnight, but try and begin to recognize discontentment (love of money) in your own attitudes when it occurs. Then, when you catch yourself being discontent, respond with Paul's advice.

2. Have the students look up Philippians 4:6 and 4:19 and summarize in their own words what Paul was saying and how it relates to resolving discontentment.

STEP 5
Trust Project (10 minutes)

Objective: To help the students see how Satan twists good things to cause us to think they are of ultimate importance. And to encourage the students to embark on a project of trusting God's answer and provision concerning something they feel they need.

1. Read this statement to the class:

> Satan often finds it more effective to deceive us by twisting the truth than by telling an outright lie. There are ways that some "things" can bring us pleasure and a certain kind of contentment, lulling us into missing what is truly worthwhile in life.

2. Invite the students to discuss the list of things the typical family needs to feel content as listed on the chalkboard in Step 1. Ask, "What is the truth about the pleasures or contentment those things can provide? How has Satan twisted that truth?"

3. After students respond to your questions, share the following:

> The basis for contentment is trust—trust in God's provision. God has promised to care for the righteous, to meet our basic needs. King David said, "I was young and now I am old, yet I have never seen the righteous forsaken, or their children begging bread" (Psalm 37:25). Similarly, Solomon declared, "The Lord does not let the righteous go hungry" (Proverbs 10:3).
>
> This does not mean that Christians will never be poor. Some of us will be poor. But there's a difference between being poor and suffering want. One can be technically poor and have what he or she needs.

A good way to learn to trust God to provide your needs is to learn to trust your parents.

4. Refer the students to Step 5 in their workbooks. Tell them to think of something they feel they need. Then suggest that they ask God to provide it for them—if it's His will. It should be something large enough that it would be difficult to get on their own at their present income level. They should write it down in their workbook and then tell their parents about it. If their parents say they should not have what they're praying for, encourage them to be content with that as God's answer. If their parents do provide the need, or if God provides in another way, then they can rejoice in that provision.

HEY, BIG SPENDER!

Background:

By this point in the course, it should be fairly obvious that there is often a big difference between the life-style advocated in Scripture and the one followed by most North American Christians. Your students, their parents and other Christians in your church may be more influenced by society's values than by Scripture when it comes to the area of spending decisions. As teacher, you must be evaluating your own financial attitudes and priorities, not presenting a model which you are not actively pursuing. It is not necessary that you have a "perfect score" in every area of your finances, but it is crucial that you be honestly exploring your own approach to spending and stewardship. Be open with your students about your own progress (and bruises) as you seek to apply Scripture to your pattern of life.

Lesson Aim:
- **To help your students discover the benefits of restraint and moderation in spending.**

Advance Preparation:

From your local library check out a copy of James Thurber's, *Further Fables for Our Time,* or some other collection that includes the tale of "The Mouse and the Money."

Supplies:

☐ Student Workbooks
☐ Bibles
☐ Pencils or pens

Getting Started (10 minutes)

As a humorous way to begin class, read "The Mouse and the Money" from James Thurber's, *Further Fables for Our Time* (New York: Simon and Schuster, 1956), pp. 109-112.

Then share the following:

> Contentment is being satisfied with God's provision; moderation is spending money sensibly, avoiding selfishness. Contentment is an inner attitude; moderation is the outward pattern of spending that results from the inner spirit of contentment. Contentment and moderation, then, usually show up together. But not always.

> A truly content Christian may not have the skills for sensible spending. And some who have sternly disciplined themselves to live within a budget (moderation) may not know the secret of contentment. They avoid the bondage of debt, but don't yet enjoy full financial freedom. To enjoy God's best, we must learn both the art of contentment and the skill

of moderation.

You have already begun to form spending habits. But in order to form them into moderate spending habits, you may need to learn to rank the importance of your purchases. One way to do this is to decide if a prospective purchase is a need, a want, or a wish. Then you can base your purchasing decisions on God's standard of moderation.

This doesn't mean that God will only meet your needs. Often, He delights in giving us comforts we "want" and even luxuries we only "wish" for. But we need to know the difference and be willing to say "no" to selfish spending.

Ask students, "Why is it important to voluntarily discipline our spending?" After several students respond, point out that moderation is necessary in order to develop a surplus. And God wants us to develop a surplus so we can: [Write these on the chalkboard.]

1. Meet our own and others' immediate needs.
2. Meet our future needs.
3. Meet others' future needs.

Before God can use your money to meet the needs He wants it to meet, you must master the skill of moderation.

This lesson explores the biblical basis of moderation, and then introduces a simple tool that can help turn you into a "smart shopper."

STEP 1
Shopping List (10 minutes)

Objective: To encourage the students to identify the wants in their life so that they can evaluate and possibly moderate them.

1. Making a shopping list of all the things they'd like to have this year should be a fun activity for your students. Let them be as creative as they want, but encourage them to be specific. For example, "A lot of money" is not very specific, but "$1,000 in the bank" is.
2. As they work on creating their list, ask for volunteers to mention one or two items on their list. It will help stimulate the thinking of others and enable you to urge specificity.

STEP 2
How to Spot a Big Spender (10 minutes)

Objective: To help the students learn to recognize the symptoms of a self-indulgent lifestyle.

1. The Student Workbook asks the students to check off any of the following statements that apply to them.

   • He buys things that aren't very useful.
   • She always shows off her things to everyone else.
   • He makes a lot of phony friends by buying them things.
   • She's constantly in the company of other big spenders.
   • His closet is full of things he hardly ever uses.
   • She can't resist a sale.
   • His money "burns a hole in his pocket."

2. Don't worry if some of your students fail to check any statements as applying to them. Go over the list verbally, and discuss with the students whether they are familiar with people who are characterized by these patterns. Young people learn much about life by observing and interpreting the behavior of others. However, discussing other people can lead to gossip. One way to avoid this is to discuss fictional persons such as characters on TV or in books.

3. Ask if any students thought of other characteristics that might identify big spenders. Some might be . . .

   • He's always first to have the newest fashion or fad.
   • She's got the most of everything, the most record albums, etc.

STEP 3
Rags, Riches, or. . .? (10 minutes)

Objective: To help the students see that God's alternative to self-indulgence isn't necessarily abject poverty but moderation.

1. Self-indulgence is one way many people get into financial bondage. God has something to say about this in His Word. Have the students use the Bible verses noted in their workbooks to answer the questions printed there.

2. Discuss the answers after they have had a few minutes to do their study. The correct answers are:

   1. C. other. The author wanted neither poverty nor riches, but life in between—moderation.
   2. Proverbs 21:17—Poverty.
      Ecclesiastes 2:10,11—Vanity and striving after the wind.
      Luke 8:14—Choked with worry.

3. The Christian should deny self, take up the cross daily, and follow Christ.

4. Agree.

STEP 4
Needs, Wants, and Wishes (10 minutes)

Objective: To help the students sharpen their discernment between needs, wants, and wishes.

1. Share the following:

> If God wants to provide our needs—but not necessarily every wish or whim—we must learn to tell the difference and develop spending habits accordingly. In this activity, you'll learn to divide your potential purchases into three categories—needs, wants, and wishes. You might discover that many things you think you need to have are merely comforts or conveniences (wants), or maybe even luxuries (wishes).
>
> Thinking of your own family, fill in the chart in Activity 4 in your workbooks as best you can. For instance, in the line marked "Car," you might fill in "shoes" as your need, "bicycle" as your want, but "motor scooter" as your wish. Or for the "Food" row you might list "Beans and rice" as your need, "Steak" as your want, and "Eat out often" as your wish.
>
> No two people will agree on every answer, but that's okay. God deals with each of us individually. One person's luxury might be another's need.
>
> Also remember that God promises to supply our needs. But often He goes further and supplies a want, or even a wish. It's not wrong to have wishes. But it's important to have the right attitude toward them. Learn to leave your wishes in God's hands—for Him to supply or withhold as He decides what's best (Matthew 6:32,33).

2. After the students have filled in the chart they should go back to their "shopping list" from Step 3 and next to each item listed, put an "N" if it's a need, a "W" if it's a want, or a "?" if it's a wish.

3. Then students should answer the remaining questions in Step 4.

STEP 5
Saying No to Selfish Spending (10 minutes)

Objective: To give the students an understanding of the advantages of moderation.

Have a group discussion of the following questions. Encourage the students to record the answers in their workbooks.

1. How can you use the "Needs-Wants-Wishes" technique as a tool to avoid selfish spending? (The "Needs-Wants-Wishes" technique can be used before you purchase something. If all your purchases tend toward "Wishes"—luxuries, you probably are being selfish. In that case you can ask God to forgive you and help you curb your spending.)

2. What do you think are the rewards of avoiding selfish spending? (A closer walk with the Lord, being sensitive to others' needs, saving money, less worry and less stress about money.)

3. What guidelines should a Christian use to determine his or her life-style? (See Proverbs 30:8,9: "Keep falsehood and lies far from me; give me neither poverty nor riches; but give me only my daily bread. Otherwise I may have too much and disown you and say 'Who is the Lord?' Or I may become poor and steal, and so dishonor the name of my God." Also, see Philippians 4:11,12: "I have learned to be content whatever the circumstances. I know what it is to be in need, and I know what it is to have plenty. I have learned the secret of being content in any and every situation, whether well fed or hungry, whether living in plenty or in want.")

DEBT ROW

Advance Preparation:

The first question in Step 3 asks, "Has God ever provided or withheld money to direct you or your family in a decision?" A sample answer is provided in this Teacher's Guide, but you should take some time to come up with your own answer to encourage the student responses.

Supplies:

- ☐ Student Workbooks
- ☐ Bibles
- ☐ Pencils or pens

Lesson Aim:
- **To help your students identify the dangers of credit so they will limit their use of credit both now and in the future.**

Getting Started (5 minutes)

Invite two students to the front of the room. Explain that the first student went to McDonalds and realized he/she forgot to bring money. A friend offered to loan this student a couple of bucks.

Ask, "Is this borrowing OK or not?" As the class responds, be sure the point is made that if the student has the money at home and pays the friend back promptly, that's merely the way good friends help each other. (However, don't make a habit of it, or your friends will get tired of bailing you out!)

Then explain that the second student wants to borrow $160 from his/her folks to buy a great new leather jacket. He/she has been wanting one for a long time, but hasn't saved the money. Now it's on sale, and the student fears losing the chance to get it at the bargain price, so he/she wants to get it right now.

Ask, "Is this borrowing OK or not? Why?" After several responses are given, point out that if the student doesn't have the money to pay back the loan, and doesn't know for sure where it will come from, that's "debt row" trouble! Whether it's a young person wanting to borrow $160 for a jacket or an adult borrowing thousands of dollars on credit cards, and from every other conceivable source, this is bondage!

This lesson will help you understand what the Bible says about credit. Hopefully, you'll be able to make wise choices in the future when you are faced with financial decisions.

STEP 1

To Borrow or Not to Borrow (10 minutes)

Objective: To open the students' thinking to the pros and cons of borrowing money.

1. Ask a volunteer to read aloud the situation that appears in the student workbook of a friend asking advice for whether he should buy a used stereo for $40 or go into debt for a new one at $325.

2. Then discuss the questions that follow. Be sure that several of the pros and cons are mentioned. Remember, going into debt would not tempt so many people if there weren't some real advantages! Some of the points under each might be as follows:

1. What would be the advantages of buying the $325 system?
   - Jim would be able to get exactly what he wanted, whereas his cousin's system may require him to give up quality or certain desirable features.
   - His cousin's stereo is obviously used and may be nearly worn out. Jim's money would be wasted if it broke down in a month. Whereas the new one would be less likely to break down and have a warranty if it did.
   - Should he ever want to, Jim could probably resell the newer system more easily and for more money than the older one.

2. What would be the advantages of buying the $40 stereo?
   - He may have a more realistic sense of how it sounds at home than the one from the store.
   - He would save a large amount of money plus the interest. While Jim's parents are offering to loan him the money at low interest, that will still increase the total cost of the stereo. (Interest is a fee charged for the use of borrowed money. It is usually set as a percentage of the amount borrowed, i.e., 10%, 12%, etc.)
   - By not having to make payments over the next year, he would be free to spend his money for other, possibly more desirable, things. One can't tell what might come up.
   - If something went wrong and Jim lost his job, he wouldn't face a financial crisis because of missing payments. He would feel freer.

3. What would be your final advice to Jim?
   - He might purchase the used stereo but also begin saving for the new one. Because of not paying interest (while earning interest on his savings), it would not cost him any more in the long run, and

he would be free from debt during the year should something more important come along or should he lose his job, etc.

STEP 2
The Range of God's Will (15 minutes)

Objective: To help the students realize that, while borrowing is not necessarily wrong, there usually are better alternatives.

1. Divide the class into small groups of three people each, and have them work together on the questions in Step 2.
2. When students finish, reconvene the class and ask for a representative from each group to share their answers. Possible answers to the questions are:

> 1a. (James 4:13-17) We do not know what will happen in the future and whether we will, for sure, be able to pay back the loan.
>
> 1b. It expresses our intention while recognizing that we don't know the future, and God may have other plans.
>
> 1c. In borrowing you are making a promise for what you will do in the future. In saving you are acting on what you intend to do while allowing for God to redirect you.
>
> 2a. (Matthew 5:42) We should be willing to give and loan to people who ask us.
>
> 2b. No. God would never encourage us to help others do what is wrong.
>
> 2c. Therefore, borrowing cannot be wrong in all circumstances.
>
> 3. (Proverbs 22:7) God's Word describes debt as a situation where the borrower becomes the servant or slave of the lender; that's not a very desirable position.
>
> 4. (Deuteronomy 15:4-6) Those who follow God's plan will not need to borrow but will be able to lend to others.
>
> 5a. (Psalm 37:21) People must repay what they borrow or they are considered wicked.
>
> 5b. (Romans 13:8) It is better to owe no one anything.
>
> 5c. (Luke 6:34,35) It is best to lend to others without expecting to be repaid.

STEP 3
God's Traffic Light (10 minutes)

Objective: To show that in our credit-ridden society, we have largely shut off a valuable channel for God's direction to us—the opportunity for Him to open or close doors by providing or withholding the provision for us to do something.

1. Share the following:

> You may have experienced a time when you sensed what God wanted you to do because of an "opened or closed door." That is, God seemed to cause everything to work out (or nothing to work out) in such a way that you felt He was leading you through circumstances. Did you ever stop and think that sometimes God uses money to open or close doors in our lives?
>
> Often, when He provides us with money for a specific and worthy purpose, we can take it as a "green light" from God to move ahead. And the same is true when God withholds money from us. When His traffic light turns red, it means stop.

2. Share this illustration or one from your own experience:

> One year, my wife and I planned to go on vacation, but we weren't able to save the money. Instead of using our credit cards, we decided we'd better just stay home. Then, a few months later, some friends called. They had rented a houseboat for a week and asked us to come along as their guests. So by waiting, we ended up having a better vacation which cost us hardly anything.

3. Work through the questions as a class exercise.

> 1. Has money ever been provided or withheld so you or your family felt God was guiding in a decision? In what ways? (Call attention to the example in the workbook or share something from your experience to stimulate group sharing.)
> 2. How could borrowing make it harder to know God's direction in a decision? (You might go ahead and do something even though God was telling you not to.)
> 3. How could borrowing demonstrate a lack of trust in God's promise to provide? (We might worry that He won't provide for us in time, or we might begin to think He can't provide, or even that He won't provide,

so we decide to get it ourselves through borrowing.)

4. How could borrowing reveal a lack of contentment? (We are not satisfied with what He does give us.)

STEP 4
Guidelines for Borrowers (10 minutes)

Objective: To help the students summarize for themselves some guidelines for borrowing.

1. Instruct class members to count off by fours, assigning the "ones" to Case Study One in the workbook, the "twos" to Case Study Two, etc. The students should work independently as they analyze their case study and then write in the space provided the suggestions they have, as well as the scriptural principle they used to formulate their suggestions.

2. Read the following three guidelines for borrowers, writing the bold-faced guidelines on the chalkboard. The students can draw from these guidelines as they formulate their suggestions for the case studies. More than one guideline may apply to each case study.

   1. **Pay it back.** Never borrow money you can't pay back on time. Only the wicked do that (Psalm 37:21).
   2. **Give God a chance to provide.** God may want to give you something debt-free! But, if you impatiently buy it on credit, you may short-circuit God's better plan (Philippians 4:6).
   3. **Keep it small if at all!** While God's Word doesn't rule out borrowing, it discourages it. Borrow sparingly, if at all (Philippians 4:19).

3. After the students have finished analyzing their case studies, read the case studies aloud and have the students share their suggestions. They should fill in the suggestions for the studies they didn't do.

Case Study One

Return to the example of your friend Jim as he says: "I'm trying to decide what stereo to buy. My cousin is willing to sell me his old stereo for $40. It's pretty good, and I've saved enough to pay cash for it. But I can get a nicer, new one for $325 and pay it off over the next year. What do you think the Lord would want me to do?"

Case Study Two

Sue wants to go to her church summer camp. But it is rather expensive and is scheduled for the first week of summer vacation. There won't be time for her to earn the money before camp. Should she try to find someone who will loan her the camp fee, hoping to pay it back after camp with a summer job? She believes God wants her to go to camp, but she wants to be careful not to ignore God's leadership and timing by borrowing.

Case Study Three

Frank is in the eighth grade and wants to trade in his old ten-speed for a new fifteen-speed mountain bike. To get the mountain bike Frank would have to (1) use all his savings as a down payment, (2) borrow $300 from his parents, (3) cut back on his spending in other areas to make the payments, and (4) take on extra neighborhood jobs in addition to his afternoon paper route.

Case Study Four

The junior high youth group has taken on the job of painting the church fellowship hall as a project. They raised most of the money and have started the work. But before they finished, they ran out of money. They need $100 for more paint to finish the job. Someone suggests asking the church board to lend them the money, which they will pay off within the year.

STEP 5
Get Out and Stay Out! (10 minutes)

Objective: To establish the steps for getting out and staying out of debt in such a way that the students can feel like it is possible and is an approach they want to follow.

1. Hopefully, your students are too young to be in debt in a formal way—credit cards, time payments, etc. However, they may have gotten into the habit of borrowing from family and friends. They are also old enough to understand something about adult finances.

   Step 5 gives them an opportunity to think through how a person can go about getting out of debt and staying out.

   After looking up the verses, tell them to arrange the steps in the order they think would be most effective.

2. Then discuss the exercise in class, asking students to explain their sequencing of the steps. (There is a right order and some reasons why.)

1. Stop borrowing and spending—Cut up all credit cards. (Proverbs 21:17—This stops the source of the problem.)
2. Develop a budget to control future spending. (Proverbs 6:6-8—This gets your spending in order.)
3. Develop a plan to pay back debts. (Psalm 37:21—Look at your budget and determine a realistic amount you can consistently pay back.)
4. Contact creditors. (Proverbs 3:27—Have your plan to pay back debts worked out and then tell your creditors precisely how you will pay them back.)

NOW, HONESTLY!

Advance Preparation:

Activity 3 suggests dividing the class into five small groups to develop mini-skits representing various passages of Scripture. If it is possible, arrange for the groups to be somewhat separated so they can work up their skits with minimum distraction.

Supplies:

☐ Student Workbooks
☐ Bibles
☐ Pencils or pens

Lesson Aim:
- To help your students understand the importance of honesty—not only in financial matters, but in other areas as well.
- To share with your students that no matter how strong a Christian may be, sometime in his or her life there is bound to come the temptation to lie.

Getting Started (5 minutes)

Read the following article that demonstrates the challenge and value of honesty in today's business world.

> "Honesty Gets Noticed," *Christian Herald,* October 1988, pp. 19,20. Reprinted by permission.
>
> Ed Moy is the field sales manager of national accounts for Blue Cross/Blue Shield of Wisconsin, a company in which he has worked for the last ten years. Seven account executives and all their support staff report to him.
>
> When I had my first offer of a "big" job, my boss asked me what the company could do to help me be successful in sales. Did I need a company car, access to the company airplane, an unlimited expense account, my own secretary? Well, my head was getting bigger and bigger, but I told him the truth: "Tom, I'd like each one of those things, but I want you to know that my ultimate boss is Jesus Christ. I want the quality of my work to please Him; you just happen to be the beneficiary. So, whether I get all or none of the things you mentioned, you can always expect me to do my best."
>
> Well, I did get that unlimited expense account as well as a company car. But when I filled out my first expense account I listed my business and personal mileage accurately. Tom called me in and said, "There must be some mistake. Your personal mileage exceeds your business mileage."
>
> I said, "That's right. It did."
>
> "But you don't understand," he said. "We salesmen don't think we are paid enough, so we pad our business mileage with all our personal mileage except for the distance from home to work." He could see that I wasn't happy, so he said, "Look, if I turned in this report this way, the difference

between your report and everyone else's could get our department audited. So, change it, or I can't sign it."

Well, that was a hard one. My ethics were impacting other people. But after I thought about it, I turned it back in without any change.

This time my boss came back and said, "You change this, and that's a direct order."

I looked him in the eye and said, "I'm a Christian, and I believe in the truth. And in the long run, I believe that telling the truth will benefit everyone. Look at it this way. If I lied on this report, how would you know that I won't lie to you when you ask me some other question? This way you'll know that no matter what you ask me, you'll get a straight answer."

It's been almost ten years since that initial interview and that discussion about honesty. Since then we've gotten along great, and today Tom is a Christian. I wasn't there to actually witness his conversion, but I'm sure that I had an impact on what he thought of Christianity.

STEP 1
It's Tempting (15 minutes)

Objective: To help the students identify how common are the temptations to be dishonest.

1. Share the following:

> Like Ed Moy, all of us have been tempted. Even Jesus was tempted (Matthew 4:1-11). Temptation can sometimes come with incredible pressures that make it hard to know what is actually the right thing to do. Think about Ed Moy's situation; it wasn't possible for him to quietly do what was right without bothering anyone else. If he filled out his expense account accurately, the cheating of his fellow workers would be obvious. They would likely get into trouble and become very angry with him.
>
> • Was doing something that might get others in trouble the best way to be a witness for Christ?
> • What alternatives did he have?

2. Let the students discuss the preceding questions, then pose the following dilemmas. After each one, allow time for them to write down their responses in their workbooks.

The Slow Leak

Your old bike still looks okay, but both tires have slow leaks. It wouldn't take much to fix them—a few bucks for new tubes—but why put money into it when you want to sell it and get a new one?

You advertised in the paper for $60, but only one person has responded. He looks it over and says that he'll give you $50.

Actually, even though you honestly think the bike is worth $60 (even with the leaky tires) you could live with $50. It will just give you enough—along with what you have already saved—to get that new trail bike you've wanted.

But then, just before your potential buyer hands you his money, he asks, "Are you sure everything is in good shape on this bike?"

What would you be tempted to say?

Pretty Good Deal

You've been trying to get to K-Mart for three days to get in on a sale of blank tapes for your cassette player. Finally you make it.

The clerk rings it up and—shock: she is charging you full price!

"But this is supposed to be on sale."

"Oh, sorry, that sale ended yesterday. $11.79."

You stand there trying to decide if you can afford it, until someone in the line behind you mumbles, "What's the hold-up?" So you fork over a twenty.

But when the clerk hands you back the change, it includes a ten dollar bill along with the ones and coins. You walk away trying to calculate whether it was really a mistake.

Yes, yes. It should have been a five with those ones. That means you did get the tapes for almost half price. Pretty good deal after all. . .or was it?

3. Go back and encourage the students to share and discuss their answers. Then lead them in responding to questions 3 and 4.

STEP 2
Why Are We Tested? (10 minutes)

Objective: To show that God can use what may seem negative to strengthen us.

1. Share the following:

> In praying to the Lord, King David said, "I know, my God, that you test the heart and are pleased with integrity" (1 Chronicles 29:17a). Think of that a moment: God tests the heart. Why would God test us? After all, He knows whether we are honest or not. So why test us? One reason God sometimes allows us to be tempted is for our own sakes. He doesn't want us to sin, but He also knows that every time we make the right choice, our character becomes stronger.
>
> It's like a car going down a muddy road. Every time the wheels go in the right direction, the ruts get deeper, and it becomes easier for the car to make the right turn next time. But when the car goes in the wrong direction, a new groove is formed. And it becomes easier and easier to make the same mistake again and again.

2. Ask a volunteer to read Luke 16:10 and summarize what it means in terms of being tested in the area of honesty.

3. Continue by asking the following questions, allowing students to repond before you share the insights given below.

- Why is this so true? (Well, because God made us, He understands how our mind works. When you do a seemingly small, honest thing—such as remind a clerk that he or she charged you fifteen cents too little on an item—your mind tells you, "Hey, you're an honest person." And your conscience lets you feel good. Your self-image as an honest person becomes stronger and stronger. And, as it becomes stronger, it becomes more and more important to you to maintain it. That creates strength of character, and strength of character is what gives you the power to be completely honest when the stakes are high.)
- When the stakes are high, what kind of person is most likely to fail to be honest? (There are actually two kinds of people who fail when the stakes are high. "The person who has been in the habit of being dishonest in small things and the person who has never been tested

and strengthened by being honest in small things."

STEP 3
Words to the Wise (20 minutes)

Objective: To explore some of the principles in Scripture concerning the importance of honesty.

1. Divide your class into five groups and assign a Scripture verse to each group with the instructions to read it and then develop a mini-skit to represent its truth. Suggest they think of a typical situation when kids their age are tempted to be dishonest.

2. As the skits are presented, write down the principle for each one on the chalkboard, encouraging the students to do the same in their workbooks.

   Group One—Proverbs 20:17. Truth: Being dishonest may seem like a good idea for a while, but your lie will eventually find you out.

   Group Two—Proverbs 20:23. Truth: Don't cheat others. Treat everyone the same.

   Group Three—Proverbs 28:6. Truth: Better to be poor and honest than rich and dishonest.

   Group Four—Luke 16:10. Truth: If you can be honest in the little things, you will be honest in the big things. If you are a liar about small things, you will be a liar about the big things.

   Group Five—Romans 13:6,7. Truth: Pay your taxes.

STEP 4
Making It Right (5 minutes)

Objective: To help your students know how to achieve a clear conscience, which is a key to future honesty and thereby financial freedom.

1. Have your students do this activity by themselves. Give them enough time to really think about their answers. The answers might be as follows:

   1. If you hide your sins, you won't succeed, but if you are sorry for your sins and stop doing wrong, people will forgive you for your wrong.

   2. Zacchaeus gave half his possessions to the poor. To the people he had cheated he gave back four times the

amount he had taken.

2. Invite further discussion. For instance, must we pay back four times the amount if we have cheated someone? (Actually, this was in full compliance with the Mosaic Law as restitution for having stolen sheep. See Exodus 22:1. For some other situations the guilty person was required to return what was stolen plus one fifth. See Leviticus 6:4,5. In Ezekiel 33:14,15 the thief is required to give back what he has taken and do no more wrong. A New Testament example is found in Paul's simple offer to repay to Philemon anything Onesimus may owe him.)

STEP 5
Guide for Prayer (5 minutes)

Objective: To allow for and encourage a personal commitment to establish a clear conscience.

1. Close with a time of silence, encouraging the students to consider the points mentioned in Step 5 in their workbooks and pray privately.
2. Offer to be available after class if anyone wants to pray or discuss some personal matter with you in greater depth.

YOU CAN'T TAKE IT WITH YOU

Advance Preparation:

☐ Rent a video of the musical, *Mary Poppins*. Run the tape about an hour and a half into the story to the point where Mr. Banks takes his children, Jane and Michael, to his place of work at the bank.

☐ Arrange to have a VCR and monitor set up in your classroom with the tape inserted and ready to play, beginning at the scene when Mr. Banks takes his children to the bank.

☐ Letter on the chalkboard or overhead:

"God wants you to save as much money as you can.
If you agree, sit on the left side of the room (◄-----).
If you disagree, sit on the right side of the room (-----►).
If you're not sure, sit in the middle."

Lesson Aim:
• To help your students understand the difference between saving and hoarding.
• To help them implement a savings plan for their own lives.

Supplies:

☐ Student Workbooks
☐ Bibles
☐ Pencils or pens

Getting Started (5 minutes)

As students arrive, call attention to the sentence and instructions on the chalkboard or overhead. Invite volunteers to explain why they agree, disagree or are unsure, alternating among the different points of view. Encourage them to be willing to move to another part of the room if someone presents a convincing argument. If everyone takes the same position, be the "devil's advocate" and raise a few issues for the other side.

After a few minutes of discussion, share the following:

> You may never have thought about this before, but God does want you to save your money. However there's a correct way to save and an incorrect way. Saving for a specific purpose is biblical (if the purpose is biblical), but stashing your money away for no apparent reason is not. That's called hoarding, and the Bible has plenty to say on that topic. 1 Timothy 6:7 says, "For we brought nothing into the world, and we can take nothing out of it."
>
> Hopefully, when you complete this lesson, you'll know how to save without hoarding.

STEP 1
A Penny Saved (20 minutes)

Objective: To help the students to identify a variety of reasons—

both good and bad—why people save money.

1. Play the video clip from *Mary Poppins*. (Assure your students that you know they are far beyond such a "childish" movie, but you want to illustrate an important point.) Stop the tape after about eight minutes, when there has been a run on the bank and the children have slipped out the door.

2. Ask: "What were the benefits the elder Mr. Dawes and other bank officers claimed would be experienced if Michael would only invest his 'tuppence' in the bank?"

   - A sense of conquest would develop.
   - His affluence would expand.
   - His money would bloom into generous amounts of credit.
   - His stature would grow.
   - His influence would expand.
   - He would be able to purchase all kinds of exotic things.

   If you do not use the video, begin the activity at this point.

3. Tell the students to consider why they think people save money. Encourage both good and bad reasons in their answers. Be as specific as possible. Have them write their answers in the spaces provided in the "coins" in their workbooks. They might include such reasons as. . .

   - Fear of the future
   - Saving for college
   - The prestige of having money in the bank
   - Saving for the purchase of a house
   - Saving for the purchase of a car
   - So they can buy things without borrowing
   - Vacations
   - Because they are tightwads and don't want to spend money
   - For new clothes

STEP 2
How Much Is Enough? (15 minutes)

Objective: To help the students understand the dangers of accumulating wealth in a non-biblical manner.

1. Have the students work alone in answering the questions in Step 2 of their workbooks.

2. When students finish the activity, spend a few minutes

discussing their conclusions. Pay particular attention to the fourth question.

1. Read Luke 12:16-21.
   a. Why did God confront the rich man? (Because the man was being greedy—hoarding his wealth).
   b. Why did the rich man hoard? (So he would feel secure and take it easy for the rest of his life.)
   c. Who else will share this rich man's fate? (Anyone who stores things for himself and neglects God.)
2. What is the danger of riches? (See Proverbs 30:7-9— Forgetting God.)
3. Read Matthew 6:19,20.
   a. What do you think these verses mean? (Saving money in banks is only temporary. But giving to the Lord's work has eternal value.)
   b. In this passage, what do you think it means to lay up treasures in heaven? (See also 1 Timothy 6:18,19—Giving money to God's work, helping others, serving God, doing what pleases God.)
4. Should a Christian save at all?
   - Read Proverbs 6:6-11. Why is the ant praised? (Because she stores up provisions for the winter.)
   - Look up Proverbs 21:20. What is the difference between the wise and the foolish man? (The foolish man uses up everything he has, but the wise man stores up a reserve.)

STEP 3
Hoarding Versus Saving (10 minutes)

Objective: To distinguish between wise saving and hoarding.

1. Ask, "How much do you think a person should save?" (According to 1 Timothy 5:8 and Hebrews 13:5, just enough to provide for the needs we have. The key issue is attitude: Are we trusting God or our savings to take care of us?)
2. Instruct the students to read through the four attitudes in their workbook which reveal that a person is hoarding.
3. Tell them to choose one of the attitudes and write in their own words how this attitude could possibly happen in their own lives.
4. Lead the class in a discussion of the following questions:

   - What do you think the difference is between wise saving and hoarding?
   - What are some good things to save money for?

STEP 4
Your Savings Plan (10 minutes)

Objective: To encourage the students to place their primary focus on storing up treasures in heaven while developing a balanced plan for earthly savings.

1. Share the following:

    Developing a biblical savings plan involves saving for specific needs. But according to Jesus, it does not involve accumulating earthly wealth for its own sake. There are two problems with hoarding.

2. Ask volunteers to look up and read Matthew 6:19 and 6:21 to discover the two main problems with hoarding. (Also see Luke 18:24.)

    - Matthew 6:19—Earthly treasure will decay, depreciate, or be stolen.
    - Matthew 6:21—Our heart will be where our treasure is, on earth rather than in heaven.

3. Share:

    However, even though "you can't take it with you" when you die, there is a way that you can send treasure on ahead to be deposited in your account in heaven. In fact, the Bible instructs us to do this by storing up treasure in heaven. But how can that be done?

4. Instruct group members to discover in the following verses how to store up treasures in heaven:

    - What should the person who has been hoarding do? (Luke 18:22—Sell everything and give the proceeds to the poor.)
    - What will happen to those who quietly help the needy? (Matthew 6:3,4—The Father will reward those who secretly help the needy.)
    - What will be the reward of faithful servants? (Matthew 25:21—The faithful servants will be placed in charge of many things.)

5. Have the students work independently as they develop a wise savings plan to provide for anticipated needs as well as to store up treasure in heaven. Circulate among them to offer encouragement and assistance where needed.

SHARING GOD'S WAY— THE TITHE

Advance Preparation:

For Activity 4, invite someone in your church who is fairly open about his or her finances to share some personal experiences with tithing. This would be most effective if the person's financial resources are or have been fairly limited, where tithing isn't a simple contribution of surplus funds. The testimony of how God sustains us when we put Him first—even when it appears as if there isn't enough—can be very powerful.

Encourage this person to share concerning specific instances when God supplied his or her needs. Inquire about the person's openness to being questioned by the students.

If you don't know whom to invite, consult your pastor or other church leaders who might know some of the most faithful tithers.

Finally, as you prepare for teaching this lesson, it is a good time to ask yourself: "Am I practicing what I'm preaching?" On the one hand, God's Word warns us that teachers will be judged more strictly (James 3:1). But on the other hand, all the blessings and promises for obedience are as much for you as for your students.

Lesson Aim:
- **To help your students understand the importance of tithing.**
- **To encourage students to begin to practice tithing from their own resources.**

Supplies:

- ☐ Student Workbooks
- ☐ Bibles
- ☐ Pencils or pens
- ☐ Glass jar filled with jelly beans, nuts or other small edible snack (which you have counted)
- ☐ Slips of paper

Getting Started *(5 minutes)*

As students arrive, instruct each one, "On a slip of paper, write your name and what you think would be a tithe of these jelly beans." Collect the guesses, select the one which came closest to the correct answer and give the jelly beans to that person.

A tithe is 10 percent of something. In ancient times it was the common measure of tribute which was given to rulers. Throughout the Bible, God's people were to give a tithe of their income to the priests at the Tabernacle or Temple. Today tithing is an important practice for the support of God's work. Many Christians don't understand tithing. They either think it's just for Jews, or they go to the other extreme and say you can't even be a Christian unless you tithe.

Tithing is not a step toward letting God rule your life; it's

something you do that says you've already taken that step.

Some people think the tithe is a nice idea, but not important for today. But what does the Bible say?

STEP 1
Is Tithing for Today? *(10 minutes)*

Objective: To discover the origins of tithing and show that it was not a practice unique to the Mosaic Law.

1. Guide the students through the following Bible study and questions.

  1. The tithe is not a legalistic idea. Over 400 years before God gave Moses the Ten Commandments, other people of faith tithed. Look up Genesis 14:18-20. Why did Abraham (Abram) deliver an offering to Melchizedek? (Abram delivered a tithe to Melchizedek because Melchizedek was a priest and Abraham was thankful that God had defeated the enemies.)

  2. Even though Christ condemned legalism, He still told us to obey the Bible. Read Matthew 23:23. Mark the box in front of the answer you believe is what Christ said when He rebuked the Pharisees for hypocrisy:

     □ a. Forget the tithe and concentrate on justice, mercy, and faithfulness.
     □ b. Practice justice, mercy, and faithfulness without neglecting the tithe.
     □ c. Do whatever seems best because you should no longer be under the Law.

     (b—Tithing was an assumed practice. The Pharisees' attitudes were wrong, but the problem wasn't tithing, it was their attitude about tithing.)

  3. Turn to Malachi 3:8—the last book of the Old Testament. What does God say avoiding the tithe is like? (Avoiding the tithe is like robbing God.)

STEP 2
Why Tithe, Anyway? *(10 minutes)*

Objective: To show that God instituted tithing for our benefit to help us remember that He is the owner and we are the stewards.

1. Share the following:

It's easy to think that we give to the church because God needs our money. In practical terms, our local church does need the support of every participant to continue its particular programs. But God actually owns everything and doesn't need anything from us. In Psalm 50:10-12 God reminds us,

"For every animal of the forest is mine,
and the cattle on a thousand hills.
I know every bird in the mountains,
and the creatures of the field are Mine.
If I were hungry, I would not tell you;
for the world is Mine, and all that is in it."

Therefore, why do we give to God?

The basic reason we give to God is for our own sake. In so doing we are reminded that He is the owner of all that we have, and we are stewards. When we try keeping it all to ourselves, we reveal a serious problem in our perspective on life. We are looking at ourselves as owners and not managers.

When we look at money and possessions that way, we inevitably look at every other aspect of our life the same way. Each of us see ourselves as "the person in charge." We begin to think of God as our Servant, there to help us from time to time when we call upon Him. Instead, we should see ourselves as God's servants, ready always to do His will. That is what it means to call Him "Lord." Lord means ruler, owner, sovereign, king.

This is why giving to God is so important. It reminds us of who He is, who we are, and what our relationship should be to the things He has allowed us to manage in His name.

But have you ever wondered why God set up a clear-cut minimum standard for giving? Why wouldn't He just encourage everyone to give whatever they wanted to give?

2. In the space provided in their workbooks, have the students write down some reasons they think God might have set up the practice of tithing. Some answers might be. . .

- So there would be a standard by which we could check our obedience.
- The people who don't believe tithing is scriptural usually give less than 10 percent, so establishing the tithe does generate a minimum amount of money back

into God's work.
- To give us a minimum to work with when planning our giving strategy.

3. Now direct the students to mark the statement that they think indicates the main purpose of the tithe. (b—The tithe is a material testimony of God's ownership of all our resources.)

STEP 3
What to Do? (15 minutes)

Objective: To give the students the chance to identify some inappropriate attitudes concerning tithing.

1. Have the students work independently on the three situations in their workbooks, writing down what they think the person should do.
2. When the students have finished writing, ask them to share their answers. Then deepen the discussion by asking the questions that appear after each situation below.

  1. Joe has a paper route each evening. His family is rather poor, and Joe must use all his own earnings for clothes, school lunches, school supplies, and bus money. After he pays all those expenses, he has very little for spending money. What should he do about giving money to the Lord's work?
     - Does God expect poor people to tithe or only those with enough extra to "afford it"? (The tithe is for our benefit. God can stretch the 90 percent to do the work of 100 percent.)
     - If he gives a tithe to the Lord's work, how will Joe have enough for what he needs? (God has promised to supply our needs if we seek and obey Him first. See Matthew 6:31-33.)
  2. Jane volunteered to spend her whole summer helping to lead neighborhood Bible clubs for younger children. She doesn't really get paid with regular wages, but from the church budget she is given a $25 per week gratuity (a "gift" of appreciation for her service). Should she tithe it? The money was already "tithed" when people gave to the church in the first place; so it's not really income, or is it? Explain your answer.
     - Look up Numbers 18:25,26. What does it say about whether God's servants need to tithe that which

has already been given as a tithe? (The Levites—God's ministers—were also expected to give a tithe of the tithes they had received for their support.)

- Again, what is the basic purpose of the tithe? (It is to help us let God rule in our lives by acknowledging that He is the owner and we are His stewards.)

3. Gary makes $10 every Saturday doing yard work for a neighbor. His take-home pay is $40.00 a month. He gives $4.00 to his church every month. In October his grandparents sent him $15.00 for his birthday. He dropped $1.50 in the church missionary fund. At Christmas, the needs of homeless children were made known to Gary in his Sunday school class. Gary felt good that he had already given his tithe and did not need to give anymore. What do you think of Gary's approach?

- Does this remind you of anyone Jesus spoke to? (Yes, Jesus scolded the Pharisees because they very legalistically tithed every little thing—like their spices—but neglected justice, mercy, and faithfulness. See Matthew 23:23).

STEP 4
Wrapping Up (20 minutes)

Objective: To learn how God has faithfully sustained and blessed someone they know who practices tithing, and to encourage the students to make a personal commitment to tithe.

1. Some of your students may be reluctant to accept the idea that giving from their limited incomes is really a good thing to do. Express your understanding of the difficulty people face when they first begin regular, proportional giving.

   Being willing to give at least 10 percent of our money to the Lord is not always easy—especially when one's resources are limited and a pattern has been established of just dropping a quarter or two in the offering plate every Sunday.

2. Invite your guest to share his or her experience concerning tithing. Then allow the students to ask questions.

3. If time remains, you may want to spend a few minutes discussing further the idea of tithing and answering any questions students may have.

4. Then encourage them to pray the following prayer of commitment that appears in their workbooks.

> Dear Lord,
>
> I know that tithing really involves letting You be the Owner over all my things. So, Lord, help me to have a healthy attitude toward giving. I want to be a cheerful giver to Your work.
>
> In Jesus' name, Amen.

SHARING FROM OBEDIENCE, ABUNDANCE, AND SACRIFICE

Background:

This lesson will probably be the most difficult of the series to convey to your students. Some of the young people will still be thinking of the tithe as mind boggling and more than they can manage. Therefore, approach this lesson as a matter of attitude, not one of expected performance. Some of your students will implement now what they learn. Others will not practice this kind of giving until the future, but the important thing is to plant the seed of this larger vision from God's Word.

Again, this is a good lesson to ask yourself whether you are practicing what you are preaching. If not, don't withhold the vision from your students, but humble yourself to be a learner, too.

Advance Preparation:

If your church or denomination has a particular channel for relief work, gather brochures or newsletters that would present the need of people in other countries for the basic necessities of life. Present this information in Step 4.

Independent Christian agencies that could provide this information are:

World Vision
919 W. Huntington Dr.
Monrovia, CA 91016

World Concern
19303 Fremont Ave., N.
Seattle, WA 98133

Food for the Hungry
7729 E. Greenway Rd.
Scottsdale, AZ 85260

Supplies:

- ☐ Student Workbooks
- ☐ Bibles
- ☐ Pencils or pens

Lesson Aim:
- To help your students understand that there's more behind the spirit of giving than "just tithing."
- To lead students to recognize that tithing is the starting point: next comes giving from obedience, abundance, and sacrifice.

Getting Started (5 minutes)

Begin class by dividing into small groups and asking them to discuss the following situation:

Suppose you have made a commitment to tithe to your church and have been doing so. But then you find out that a friend's family is having severe money problems, and your friend won't be receiving any Christmas presents. Even though you have already given your tithe, should you do more?

After students talk about the situation, invite volunteers to report on their conclusions. Then point out that once a person is committed to tithing, God may ask that person to take the next steps—giving out of obedience, giving from abundance, and giving as a sacrifice.

STEP 1
Sharing from Obedience (10 minutes)

Objective: To help the students to understand that sharing from obedience means sharing with those in need above the tithe because of an attitude of Christian compassion and mercy.

1. Continue sharing:

> Sharing from obedience means sharing above your tithe in obedience to God's Word. God will show you people who need help as you begin to recognize your responsibility to help them.
>
> In Matthew 23:23, Jesus scolded the Pharisees because, even though they carefully tithed such minor things as the herbs from their garden, they "neglected the more important matters of the law—justice and mercy and faithfulness." While He affirmed their tithing, He said that the Law called them to go further.
>
> In verse 25, He said that they were "full of greed and self-indulgence." Obedience to God calls for something more than legalistic observance of tithing, because it is possible to technically tithe to God and be cruel to people in need.

2. Ask three volunteers to read aloud Matthew 25:31-40. Have one person read the narrative, the second read the words of the King, and the third read the words of the righteous people.

Instruct the students to think about this passage for a few minutes, then write down in their own words what they think the passage means.

3. Next, invite group members to read aloud what they wrote.

STEP 2
Sharing from Abundance (10 minutes)

Objective: To help the students realize that if they have more than they need, it is probably because God has entrusted it to them so they can meet the need of someone else.

1. Teach the following:

> Sharing from abundance is difficult for many to do because they like the feeling of having a little nest egg, "just in case." What if you've been saving for a new skateboard and you discover someone else can't get some needed new shoes. Would you be willing to take some of your savings and meet that need? That's giving from abundance. It's the attitude that says, "Others have little, and I have so much—I'm willing to help others."
>
> We've already discussed that saving your money is biblical. But, one of the reasons to save is so you can share with others when a need arises.

2. Ask a volunteer read aloud 2 Corinthians 8:13-15.
3. Discuss as a class the question about equality, encouraging the students to fill in their workbooks as comments are shared.

> 1 . What do you think Paul was talking about when he used the word, "equality"? (In most cases, God uses people to meet the needs of other people. Therefore, if someone has extra, God has given it to them for the very purpose of meeting someone else's need. This kind of give and take is absolutely crucial within the Christian community.)

4. Allow a few minutes for students to write out a few practical ideas of the ways they could give out of their abundance. Suggest a few ideas to help them get started. . .

   • Whenever I get extra money for gifts, I'll give half of it to someone needy.
   • I'll baby-sit for a needy family and not charge.
   • I'll tutor a student at school and either not charge or give the money to someone needy.

STEP 3
Sharing from Sacrifice (15 minutes)

Objective: To inspire the students with a vision of the mature trust in God required give up something they need—trusting that

God will care for them—to provide for the greater need of someone else.

1. Share the following:

> Sacrificial giving means giving up a "need" to help someone who may have even greater needs. Jesus describes this attitude in Luke 21:1-4:

> "And He looked up and saw the rich putting their gifts into the treasury. And He saw a certain poor widow putting in two small copper coins. And He said, 'Truly I say to you, this poor widow put in more than all of them; for they all out of their surplus put into the offering; but she out of her poverty put in all that she had to live on.'"

> This is an example of sacrificial giving.

2. Ask students to explain why the widow's gift pleased Christ more than the larger gifts from the rich. (The widow's contribution pleased Jesus because she gave everything she had and in so doing demonstrated a profound trust that God would still meet her needs.)

> You might say, "But if I give up something I need, won't I end up suffering, too?"

> That's a good question, and Jesus answered it directly when He said, "Seek first his kingdom and his righteousness, and all these things will be given to you as well" (Matthew 6:33). The "things" He was referring to were the basics of life—the food and drink and clothing that we all need.

> This does not mean that Christians will never be poor. Some of us will be poor. But there's a difference between being poor and suffering because one doesn't have something that is essential. One can be technically poor and have all the money or things one needs.

> God's promise also does not suggest that we can be lazy and expect God to feed us. Paul set down the rule: "If a man will not work, he shall not eat" (2 Thessalonians 3:10). Laziness is not consistent with righteousness.

> But God has promised to care for the righteous, to meet our basic needs. King David said, "I was young and now I am old, yet I have never seen the righteous forsaken or their children begging bread" (Psalm 37:25). Similarly, Solomon declared, "The Lord does not let the righteous go hungry" (Proverbs 10:3).

3. Ask students to consider the following examples:

   - **Sharing from obedience.** Suppose your grandmother gives you $25 for your birthday to be used for a new watch. Sharing from obedience would be like giving $10 to a friend who has a need and then looking for a cheaper watch.
   - **Sharing from abundance** would be like giving your friend the $25 and continuing to use your old watch.
   - **Sharing from sacrifice.** This would be like giving your friend the $25 even though you really needed the watch and didn't know where you would get one. You would be giving up a need for the sake of meeting someone else's greater need.

STEP 4
My Sharing Plan (20 minutes)

Objective: To encourage the students to develop a sharing plan that stretches them to new levels of faith.

1. Present two or three current examples of great need by people in other parts of the world as reported in the brochures or newsletters of Christian mission or relief organizations. Use this, not to solicit funds for those specific causes, but to remind the young people of their privileged position of abundance in contrast to the great need of other people.

   Some students may not be ready to do more than contribute their tithe to the Lord—even this is far more than many Christians do. However, they still need a vision of what might be called the more advanced levels of Christian stewardship. Without pressuring them, you can invite them to try the Lord and prove His faithfulness. As God said in Malachi 3:10, "Test Me now in this, . . . if I will not throw open the floodgates of heaven and pour out so much blessing that you will not have room enough for it."

2. Allow time for the students to work out a specific plan to help them become better stewards. The workbook asks them to estimate their monthly income and from that their tithe. Then it suggests the following format for further giving.

   - **Obedience:** To help meet the needs of people in greatest need, I will set aside $_____ of my income for sharing.
   - **Abundance:** If I receive unexpected income, I will set aside _____ percent of that surplus for sharing. I will

use the rest of my surplus for _____

_____

- **Sacrifice:** In order to share with others who have less, I am willing to do without the following items in my usual monthly budget:

_____

_____

WHO DESERVES HELP?

Advance Preparation:

Collect a variety of fund-raising appeals that come in your mail (or to your church's office) to use in Getting Started. (You might want to ask a few others at church to contribute ones they receive.) Also check through several Christian magazines for various advertisements that appeal for help of various kinds—needy children overseas, famine relief, etc.)

Optional activity in Step 5: If you choose to do this activity, you will need blank paper, magazines, scissors, crayons or markers, pens, pencils, glue, etc.

Field trip option: Check out the possibility of taking your students on a service project to help make or serve a meal at a local shelter for the homeless or a rescue mission. Things to consider: communicate with parents about details of the project; arrange transportation; enlist additional adults as drivers and chaperones (at least one adult for every six young people).

Supplies:

☐ Student Workbooks
☐ Bibles
☐ Pencils or pens

Lesson Aim:
- To communicate that being a good steward means helping some and not helping others.
- To help your students learn how to discern who to help.

Getting Started (5 minutes)

Pass around a variety of fund-raising appeals that you have collected (see Advance Preparation). Then, using a chalkboard to record responses, brainstorm with the class a list of appeals for help that they (or their family) have encountered. For example: Have they been stopped on the street by someone asking for a quarter? Have they seen pleas for funds on television? Have people come door-to-door, soliciting funds?

Ask, "How did you react to these appeals?"

Share the following:

> Now that we've learned the principles of giving, it's important to decide who deserves our help. Contrary to popular opinion, God does not direct us to help out everyone who knocks on our door or stops us on the street or pleads for our money over TV. This lesson should help you learn how to know who to help.

STEP 1
Whom the Bible Says to Help (15 minutes)

Objective: To direct students to Scripture for some guidelines on whom to help.

1. Instruct students, working in pairs, to look up the six Scriptures listed in their workbook and match each to the appropriate type of giving listed on the right.

Answers:
1. Malachi 3:10a   (D) Funding church programs.
2. 1 Timothy 5:17,18   (A) Support for ministers.
3. 2 Corinthians 8:1-5   (E) Sharing with Christians.
4. 1 Timothy 5:8   (B) Helping needy relatives.
5. Matthew 19:21   (F) Giving to the poor.
6. Philippians 4:15-17   (C) Supporting missionaries.

As students finish, read the references and ask volunteers to give the answers. If students have questions about the meaning of a passage, take a few minutes to discuss it together. Then say:

> Each of these kinds of giving pleases God. And, as Jesus said, "Whatever you did..., you did for me" (Matthew 25:40). Giving as God wants us to give is counted as giving to Him.

2. Now ask students to think of people they know who fit each of these six categories. If possible, encourage them to write down individuals by name. Start by giving some of your own ideas.
3. Ask a volunteer to read 2 Thessalonians 3:10 aloud. Allow a few minutes for students to write answers to the two questions in their workbooks; then discuss their answers. You may want to comment as follows:

> Of course, the difficult part is that people who won't work usually offer all kinds of excuses for why they "can't" work or can't find a job.
>
> Paul's counsel to the Thessalonians was to a church where it was fairly easy to know whether the people in question could work but were just refusing to do so. Many times when we are approached by a panhandler or someone else wanting help, we don't know the facts, so it is usually better to err on the side of generosity.

STEP 2
Sharing with Your Family (5 minutes)

Objective: To encourage students to realize they can give to the members of their family, including ways other than giving money.

1. Helping out their families is probably a new idea to many of your students. But concern for others in the family can help renew family relationships. Emphasize helping in ways other than money, though not excluding it.

   Introduce the activity by saying:

   > Sharing with your family means more than just your parents, brothers, and sisters. It also includes aunts, uncles, cousins and grandparents who might need help. This might seem like a strange concept to you, especially if you're used to having your own needs met all the time by these people.
   >
   > But don't forget that giving doesn't always have to involve money. Is there someone you can think of in your family who has a need? It may be a distant relative you barely know who might appreciate letters. Do you have an older relative who could use some help or just a regular visit? Is one of your cousins trying to raise money toward a special project? Pray about helping this individual. Ask your parents for ideas.

2. Allow a few minutes for students to consider and write down one family member or relative they'd like to help, and how. If several students seem stuck, brainstorm some possibilities as a class. Examples:

   - Volunteer to do chores for Grandma.
   - Run errands for my aunt.
   - Help my younger brother in math.
   - Contribute to my cousin's short-term mission project.

STEP 3
Sharing with the Body of Christ (10 minutes)

Objective: To discuss ways students can help fellow believers in the church.

The questions in the workbook can be done either individually or as a class discussion. If you do the activity as a group, proceed as follows.

1. Ask a volunteer to read aloud 1 John 3:17,18, then ask: "What does God decide if we have a surplus and find a fellow Christian in need, but don't help him or her?" (If someone does not help a Christian brother or sister in need, the love of God is

not in that person.)

2. Question 2 may be difficult for students to share about, even if they're aware of a situation when they didn't meet a need when they could have. Be prepared to share an example from your own experience or the following situation a young person reported:

> "Last year for my birthday, my grandparents gave me $50. I didn't really have a specific use for the money, and I had gotten quite a few gifts from family and friends. Someone at the church had a flat tire and needed $50 to replace it. Everyone prayed that the $50 would be provided. I knew about my $50, but I felt that it was gift money and I shouldn't give it away. I also felt that maybe it was an adult problem, not mine.
>
> "Still, I felt kind of selfish and 'un-Christian.' But I just couldn't let go of the money."

3. Question 3 asks students to recall a time when they were able to meet another's need, and it may be easier to share about. Be careful not to let this become bragging or comparing. Still, it can be encouraging for young people to share ways they can help others. An example:

> "I baby-sat a few months ago and received more than I expected. (I got $10 total.) I had planned to buy material to make a dress. When I got home, my little sister was in tears because she had just discovered she was $10 short for something she was planning to buy. I just reached in my pocket and gave her my $10.
>
> "I felt great. I felt like I had really done something nice for my sister. Our relationship got closer after that event."

STEP 4
Hey, Mister Christian! (15 minutes)

Objective: To portray through a skit some familiar excuses for not helping.

1. Assign the parts of the Poor Mother, Teenager, Unemployed Worker, and Narrator to four of the students. Take on the part of Mr. Christian yourself.

2. With your "cast", read through the skit, then use the following questions to stimulate discussion:

> 1. To whom did Mr. Christian most often pass the buck?

(To the pastor; he was the one who was expected to do it all—pray, visit, etc.)

2. Should Mr. Christian meet all these needs himself? (Not necessarily; but he should be willing to get personally involved, if he can. If he can't, he should see that the needs get met another way, and are not just brushed aside.)

3. What other responses might be possible that would help meet needs but share the load?

4. In what way is helping people with real needs a form of evangelism? (People whose needs are met by Christians experience God's love through them, and may become open to the Gospel.)

STEP 5
You Did It to Me! (10 minutes)

Objective: To help students realize that giving to people in need is really giving to God. Also to give some guidelines for discerning which organizations are deserving of financial gifts.

1. Ask four volunteers to read aloud Matthew 25:34-46. Assign one person to be the Narrator, another to be the King, a third to be the righteous people and the fourth to read the words of those who are banished.

2. Guide students in answering the two questions in their workbooks.

1. What are some reasons God might want us to help the needy? (To demonstrate God's love to others. To demonstrate our love to God. To be God's hands in healing and helping. Etc.)

2. What are the consequences if we don't? (We are really rejecting God. We show we don't really love God. People don't experience God's love through us. Etc.)

Optional Activity:

Divide the class into five groups. Assign each group one of the phrases from Matthew 25 listed in their workbooks. Instruct them to illustrate it creatively, using the blank paper, magazines, scissors, crayons or markers, pens, pencils, glue, etc., which you have provided. They might make a collage of magazine clippings, write a poem, draw a sketch, use colors to represent feelings, or whatever they choose.

Sometimes "No" Is Okay

3. In closing, share the following:

> Obviously we cannot give to every worthy organization or person in need, but we should do what we can. Many charitable requests are deserving of your gifts. But some are not. Don't feel guilty about saying "no" to some requests for money if you don't feel the organization will use it properly.

4. Ask volunteers to read aloud the seven questions to ask that help them discern worthy recipients of their giving. Do the students have any questions about how to know whether a need or organization is deserving of help? Can they think of any examples they think are deserving? Undeserving? What are their reasons?

Field Trip Option

If possible, arrange to take your students on a service project to help make or serve a meal at a local shelter for the homeless, soup kitchen, or rescue mission. If it can be done in the same week as this lesson, all the better. Pass out the necessary information for students to share with their parents. Include some time afterwards for students to share their impressions and feelings about the experience.

ON TO FREEDOM

Advance Preparation:

Step 4 suggests celebrating all the hard work you've done together as a class with snacks. You can decide to treat the class yourself—or, if the class is large, ask some of the students (or their parents) to help out by bringing paper goods, snacks, drinks, etc.

Supplies:

- ☐ Student Workbooks
- ☐ Bibles
- ☐ Pencils or pens
- ☐ Paper strips the size of bumper stickers
- ☐ Felt markers
- ☐ Masking tape

Lesson Aim:
- To review the entire study on finances, and answer any questions your students may still have.
- To help students think through their own spending habits—how they've been and how they'd like them to be.

Getting Started (5 minutes)

As students arrive, give them a strip of paper and a felt marker to use in making a "bumper sticker" with some good advice about using money. Encourage them to think of ideas they have gained during this course, then try to write a short slogan or statement about one of those ideas. Have students mount the finished strips around the room as they finish them.

Share the following as students complete their slogans:

> You've probably heard a lot of new ideas since you began this Bible study—some of which you have implemented in your Christian walk already and some that you haven't, at least not yet.
>
> This lesson should help you review the principles you learned earlier, and help you make decisions about which ones you feel ready to start practicing in your own life.

STEP 1
The Growing Edge (10 minutes)

Objective: To help students think through which financial concepts studied in this course have been most important to them personally.

1. Read through the three questions in this activity.

    1. What is the most important concept you've learned in this course?

    2. What is one way you are already using something you learned in this study?

3. What would you like to be doing that you learned in this course, but haven't started putting into practice yet?

2. Allow students five minutes to answer the questions in their workbooks. If students need to review the concepts, encourage them to leaf through the previous lessons and activities they've already done.

3. When most students seem to be done writing, let them read one of their answers. You might ask, "Chris, what is one way you are already using something you learned in this course?" Don't force any answers; keep the sharing light and voluntary. Affirm that the responses will be different for different students.

STEP 2
Your Next Step (10 minutes)

Objective: To review the various principles that lead to financial freedom, and to make sure students understand the implications; and to encourage students to make a commitment to apply what they've learned in the Bible study to their lives.

1. Ask each student to choose one of the "Ten Steps to Financial Freedom" and write a paragraph of why they feel that step is important—or an example of what that step might mean when applied to real-life situations.

2. After several minutes, invite volunteers to read their paragraphs aloud.

3. Then encourage your students, working individually, to (1) write out (or circle) the step they need to take next in their own journey toward financial freedom, and (2) write out how this step would make a difference in the way they live.

STEP 3
Where the Money Goes (25 minutes)

Objective: To guide students in charting their own personal income and expenditures during a typical month—both how it has been, and how they'd like it to be.

1. Explain the following:

Many people—adults as well as young people—have good intentions about finances, but when it comes to handling their money on a week-to-week basis, they don't have a clear idea of what happens to it. Financial freedom means being in charge of your money, rather than it being in charge of you. That means it's important, first of all, to have a good idea of how you actually spend your money, and second, to make a plan—called a budget—of how you'd like to use your money.

2. Ask the students to look over the two charts in Step 3 of their Student Workbooks. Tell them to estimate as best they can how much income they receive in a typical month. This might come from several sources: an allowance, extra chores, baby-sitting or other jobs, gifts from grandparents, money from parents designated for specific expenses, etc.

3. Then tell students to estimate the amount they usually spend on the various categories listed. Do the income and expense totals match? Obviously, not all the categories will apply to everyone. Amounts that junior high young people have to manage may vary widely. They should resist comparing themselves with others.

4. Encourage students to fill out the chart again, except this time to think ahead and make a plan for how they'd *like* to use their money, based on the concepts and principles they've learned in this course. Again, do the totals match?

Encourage each student to set up his or her own spending/saving/giving plan, based on his or her personal financial situation and goals.

Note: If students have a difficult time estimating how they spend their money, suggest that they keep track of their expenditures for a month. This can be done simply by writing down each day the amount and what it was spent for.

At the end of the month, they can add similar things together: a pair of socks, sunglasses, and a tee-shirt would be added together under "clothes." Bus fare, school lunches, and notebook paper would be lumped together under "school," and so on. They might be surprised where the money actually goes! Remind them:

> To make a new plan for the money that's flowing,
> You need to first know where your money's been going!

STEP 4
My Covenant of Stewardship (10 minutes)

Objective: To summarize the important Scriptural principles studied in these lessons in the form of a class covenant.

1. As a fitting close to the thirteen sessions you have spent

together studying God's principles of financial freedom, participate with your students in reading a "Covenant of Stewardship" from the workbooks.

Assign each student (or small group) one or more of the statements from God's Word—excluding the first two and the concluding one.

- Instruct the students to write a response to their assigned verse, expressing a specific thing they can do to show awareness of the truth of that verse. Call attention to the two Sample Responses.
- You might want to stand together, acknowledging the solemn, corporate pledge you are making to obey God in managing His resources.
- As teacher, you can read the part marked "God's Word," or select a good reader who can speak out.
- The students would then read the "Response" they wrote. (Or, divide the class into a speaking choir, with half reading "God's Word," and the other half reading each "Response.")

2. Now, as a reward for all the hard work you've done together, why not celebrate with some doughnuts and cider?